THIS AMERICAN LIFE SEF!

The Life of African Immigrants in America

Rudolf Ogoo Okonkwo

Jointly published by
Noirledge Limited, under its Winepress Publishing imprint
and Irokopost Media Group Inc., Rosedale, NY 11422

Noirledge Limited
13, Elewura Street, off Lagos Bypass, Challenge, Ibadan
Tel: +234 809 816 4359 | +234 805 316 4359
Email: press@winepress.pub | www.winepress.pub

Copyright © Rudolf Ogoo Okonkwo, 2018
Rudolf Ogoo Okonkwo asserts the moral right to be identified as the author of this work.

ISBN: 978-0-9768354-6-2.
A catalogue record for this book is available from the National Library of Nigeria.

All rights reserved. No part of this publication may be reproduced, stored in or introduced into a retrieval system, or transmitted, in any form or by any means, electronic, mechanical, photocopying, recording or otherwise, without prior permission in writing from Irokopost Media Group Inc. and the copyright owner. Any unauthorised distribution or use of this publication may be a direct infringement of the author's and publisher's rights, and those responsible may be liable in law accordingly.

Cover Illustration: Solomon Isekeije
Cover Design: Tokunbo E. Olujide
Book Design: Servio Gbadamosi
Typesetting: www.noirledge.com

Acclaim for This American Life Sef!

"*This American Life Sef!* yields a mixture of laughter and tears in an almost equal proportion. So true, so terrifying."
—Niyi Osundare,
Distinguished Professor of Literature
University of New Orleans

"Rudolf Okonkwo, whether he's writing on Nigerians' idiosyncrasies, political attitudes, or arcana, is dangerously funny and irresistibly addictive. Read this small gem of a book and understand what Nigerians mean when they say, 'laughter will kill me'. After the laughter, though, comes pensive, self-enlarging thought. If Rudolf were a vitamin, doctors would recommend a daily dose of him to all of us, period!"
—Okey Ndibe, author, *Never Look an American in the Eye*

"*This American Life Sef!* is a worthy addition to our growing canon of immigrant tales. It is sensitively written, insightful and engaging. It evokes sadness and inspires mirth, all on the same page. Rudolf Ogoo Okonkwo has more than made up for his inattentiveness on that plane journey from long ago."
—Molara Wood, *The Guardian Newspaper*

"Not a few will be offended by Rudolf Okonkwo's dare to reveal a different picture, and one that is not in the least paradisiacal, from the one they have developed and like to retain of life in America... On the surface, this book is deceitfully simple but underneath this apparent simplicity lies strong currents which are bound to knock the reader about. The culture shock contained therein is as severe as that in James Baldwin's *Notes of a Native Son*."
—Uchenna Franklin Ekweremadu

"This brilliantly summarizes the dilemma of living in a strange culture that offers material benefits but no cultural or spiritual

grounding to our youngsters."
—*AU Citizen*

"This is so important that it should be sent to all secondary schools and markets in Nigeria. It is apt for America and true for Europe: Italy, Greece, Spain, UK: even Sweden and Germany. No better place than a functioning Fatherland!"
—*Denis Ezieme*

"This is a harsh reality check. It mirrors the life of a whole bunch of us in the diaspora now—and going forward."
—*Stan Okey Odume*

"The Rudolf trademark: intellect, wisdom, satire, humour, comedy, bitter truth, and fiction all rolled in an amazing cocktail..." —*Anonymous*

"Man, you got me thinking. What you narrated above is the agony most people living in the West go through, even though most of us wouldn't admit it."
—*Emeka, London*

"This is indeed a classic. It made me laugh to nuts in public. Ironically, it is so true, even for those of us that are not yet living in America."
—*Oye*

"Yeah... It's hilarious, but it's also quite true—which is the tragedy."
—*Gbosa Express*

"Rudolf, you are a comedian. This is film stuff, and with a brilliant team, this will have the box-office bursting and people rolling off their seats. At the same time the actual story and your heartache will not be overlooked. This is brilliant stuff! Well written."
—*Ms. Omayeli Odeli*

Dedication

To the people who made my American journey smooth:
Samson Okafor and Anuli Ezumba-Okafor,
Pius Airewele and Rose Egbuiwe

Contents

Preface	11
Introduction to the New Edition	13
Introduction	15

ESSAYS

I'll Marry When I Want	19
Saving Mama Udoka	25
Just Before You Kill Your Wife	33
This American Life	37
Our Children Are Coming	42
This American Life Sef! II.	46

SHORT STORIES

A Kernel for a Fowl	53
The Butcher, the Surgeon and I	64
The Attack of the Dwarfs	88

INTERVIEW

Extract from an Interview with Sun Newspaper's Henry Akubuiro	103
Acknowledgements	113

"We don't receive wisdom; we must discover it for ourselves after a journey that no one can take for us or spare us."
— Marcel Proust (1871-1922)

Preface

Every sojourner owes a debt
To the roads, the rivers
And the spirits that pilot the stars
But the debt that lives in whispers
Is the debt of return.
It's one debt that is never forgiven
Not by bankruptcy,
And not by death.
So what happens to the debt,
When the sojourner cannot return?
Does it morph into a myth of thunder subdued?
What happens to the journey
When desires mutate the mission?
Does it trim the wings and let the treasure be?
What happens to the home
When wants alter the DNA of its bones?
Does it turn into a nursery
For children of the great beyond?
Each sojourner answers these questions
In their own ways.
Some with tears dripping down their cheeks
Some with honey on the edges of their smiles
Whatever your story is
The heels that embarked on a journey
Has earned three privileges:
The right to sing and dance
The power to order the mouth to recall
And the guts to hold up a mirror.

Introduction to the New Edition

I decided to put this book together as a complementary book to a tour of the US that I embarked on with Adeola Fayehun of Keeping It Real with Adeola in December 2015. The theme of the tour was, "This America Sef Tour." So, it fitted well.

What I did not know was that it would speak to so many people in so many ways.

The first print run has been exhausted. There was no time to update it before the second print had to be done to meet demands. As the second print runs out, I felt it would not be fair to go for a third print without an update—after all, it has been two years since the first edition. That is the reason for this second edition.

I have decided to add a new introduction to the second edition. I also added a part two of the core essay, "This American Life Sef!" It takes the story further as our sojourner gets older, what options are there for him or her?

At the end of the book, I also added an extract from an interview I granted the Sun newspaper in Nigeria. It will give an insight into the thinking behind the book and some questions that have been in the minds of readers all over the world.

Moved by the reactions I have received in the last year, I have added a new short story, "The Attack of the Dwarfs" for your reading pleasure.

It has been a great blessing getting feedback from readers like you. And I immensely thank you.

Rudolf Ogoo Okonkwo
Rosedale, New York City
May, 2018

Introduction

I was struggling to snap my seat belt in place without looking like a Bushman but the man sitting next to me in the plane could see the orbs of sweat forming on my forehead.

"Your first time traveling abroad?" he asked.

I nodded.

Seat belts in a plane are not different from the ones in cars. But I did not know that because in my father's Peugeot 504 L, we never used the seat belts. It was not because we didn't care about safety. It was just that when nine people are squeezed into a car like that, there is no room for seat belt protocol.

I eventually managed to get it in. I wiped the sweat off my face and buckled up for the dreaded plane's take off that I had been warned about. With my heart pounding, this man who would not mind his business asked me; "Where are you going? What for? When are you coming back home?"

I felt like smacking the man. I was pissed off more by the question about when I would be returning back to Nigeria. I cannot recall now what I said to him but I remembered him telling me that he was tired of living in Houston, Texas, and was finishing plans to permanently relocate to Nigeria.

I doubt if I spoke to him again throughout the flight to London. From London, I travelled on to Switzerland. Chances are that he told me things about America that I did not pay attention to. Probably the same kind of things I heard from relations who lived in America and others I met while I was living in London. These were things I dismissed with a wave of the hand before they take root in a mind that was determined to get to America.

Because of that man in the plane and many before and after him, I could not feign ignorance like Andy in the classic Nollywood movie, *Living In Bondage*. When he finds out that his friend, Paulo's much admired get-rich-quick scheme entailed sacrificing his wife to the oracle, he laments, "Paulo didn't explain this thing very well to me."

This is my little way of finishing the job Paulo did not do well. This is my little contribution to the desire by many to shine a light on this American life.

Rudolf Ogoo Okonkwo
Rosedale, New York City
December, 2015

Essays

I'll Marry When I Want

In less than four years in America, I have seen more dead men walking than I had seen in all my years in Nigeria. Everywhere I look, I see children of Africa who have become ghosts of their former selves. The noisy ones are sheer empty vessels. The dumb ones are experiencing shock. A distorted image of life and perception had transformed the Africans in America into a pathetic lot. There are more of them struggling to retain their sanity than there are those who are struggling to save their souls. The only gap between their American dream and their American nightmare is their American experience.

One Saturday in March, I watched a Nigerian woman who lived in a high-rise housing complex in Massachusetts assemble her family laundry and bundle them into the laundry room on the 8th floor. The crowded room was full of residents who had gathered to do their laundry. The Nigerian woman noticed that white couples came to the laundry room together; the man helping out in carrying the clothes, sorting them out and subsequently folding them after washing. Only African women had to come alone to the laundry, do all the tasks involved, only to return to their apartments to cook food for their husbands, who all the while were sitting on the couch flipping channels in search of violent sports and naked women.

The African man in America is confused. Those who are trying to be Africans in their homes are forced to be Americans outside their homes, while those who are pretending to be

Americans in their homes, are daily reminded by the reality outside that they fall short of that title, in effect, raising so many questions and creating so many conflicts. For instance, is a career-minded African wife of an African man, with a 9-5 job obligated to carry out the typical duties expected of an African housewife? When the need arises, who is going to sacrifice the time to take care of family problems - the man or the woman? Who is paying the bills and how much of that translates into veto power in family matters?

I once pointed out this perennial struggle of the African man to an African woman. She instantly barked at me. Her question was, how come when an African marries an "akata" or a "fat white trash", he knows how to behave—how to do the laundry, cook, clean the house, take the baby to the hospital, pick up the baby from the day care, etc. while the wife sits at home watching the *Jerry Springer Show*; but as soon as he escapes from the American woman, he instantly remembers how to be an African man? Because he got himself a slave as wife?

I met this Nigerian man recently. He had spent a greater part of his 19 years in America working at one nursing home after another. He has become an expert at changing old women's diapers. Nothing is too gross for him to handle. He lives in a huge nice house, one that would make you mistake him for a brain surgeon. And of course, he drives a big expensive car. But deep inside him, the man has died. He had to put up the external appearance to beef up his non-existent self-esteem. Unlike most people who love to care for the old, the sick, and the mentally challenged, this man is there just for the money. His favourite expression is that his paycheque "doesn't smell like shit". In his heart of hearts, he hates every minute of his job. But until his dignity is restored, he cannot in any way function as either a real African or an unhyphenated American.

But don't ever try to use this story to buy the sympathy of the African woman. Unlike the African woman back home, the

African woman in America faces a greater expectation from the African society. She too receives letters from home. And like all those letters, they are asking for favours, like money for hospital bills, ticket to Germany, school fees, etc. She is under the kind of pressure that a typical married African woman at home would not face. She is in effect expected to be a provider as well as the mother of her husband's children. And in this society where the instruments of law favour women, the African woman is stunned that she has remained downtrodden.

What kind of support does the African man need from the African wife in America? A phone bill that is as long as the River Nile? A credit card bill that runs up and down Mount Kilimanjaro? A third car payment for the additional van, the symbol of the soccer mom generation? Or is it the yearly mother in-law visit? Or the bringing over of the wife's sister and/or brother to school in the United States? If the head of the household must bear the full responsibility, what happens to the privileges which the American society does not recognize?

When does one tag an African woman wild? Is it when she threatens to sue him for divorce and take her husband to the laundry, as they say? Or is it when she calls the cops and accuses her husband of attempting to rape her? Does buying Victoria's Secret count? The most intriguing fact about the African woman in America is their class. Whether they are "imported" or "exported", the African woman in America belongs to the best of the best. If they fail to stand on their feet for what they believe in this free country, what hope is there for the African woman at home? Have you heard what follows when, in the heat of an argument, an African woman tells her husband, "This is America and..."

On my prompting, an African friend of mine bought flowers for his African wife. By the end of Valentine's Day, the flowers had been squashed to death on the man's body. The woman later told me it was the last time she would ever try to make a romantic candle-light dinner. Shame on you Africans, she said. Where is the love? Is America so full of only Okonkwos? What happened to the Njoroges? I understand when an African marriage fails because an African man wants to videotape himself making love to his wife. But to insist on calling your wife Mama Tayo in America where no woman wants to be old is classic folly.

The last time I checked, the African woman is still trying to be African. She is gossiping about other women and their husbands. She is assessing whose Mercedes is bigger. She is quarrelling, even fighting. Have you seen them at baby showers? It is a lioness' den. If you are a man, an African man, you don't want to be anywhere near. Despite America's craze for skinny women, the African woman seems not to be particularly worried. Some punish themselves with visits to the gym. Additional burden, you might say, but so far, Holland Blocks and blouses still fit. But as more and more Ally McBeals of Africa emerge, trouble as huge as yellow skin fever in the 70s brews.

I once asked an African man what contribution he would say he made to the American society after 20 years in America. He snapped, "I did not come here to contribute any shit. I came here to make money." He has a house in his hometown of Mbaino in which he would never spend up to 200 days from now till he dies. He had been sending money home ever since he started working, and the demand has only increased. His children understand bits of his mother tongue but cannot say water without pronouncing the letter t. To him, he is accomplished.

I respect the man's idea of accomplishment. But my idea is a little wider. I want to marry who I want, when I want and how I want. I want to graduate from preaching. I want to advance to that difficult practical level where I have to implement what I preach. I want to try to establish that ideal African family we have been fighting for. Because that is the frontline of this battle of America, their America.

The other day, looking at America, their America and all these battles that African men and women face in this land, I e-mailed the African woman I hope to marry. In my letter I stated my creed. Here are extracts:

"My dear, I am writing this from the very bottom of my heart. I was touched yesterday when you said I had changed. It wasn't because you were right, rather, it was because I had been debating the very opposite... While a part of me may be half-dead, a significant part is still half born. I don't know what is dying but I do know what is being born. The labour of its birth has been going on for so long. Sometimes, I cry for a stillbirth, rather than an endless pain of labour without any fruit.

"...Sometimes I see myself as firewood. I see myself trapped inside the three-legged metal that holds the pot in the chimney area of the kitchen. I notice the coal underneath me. I feel their warmth - their simmering. I could see Mama picking the grains of rice, washing them, and getting them ready for cooking. But being a very dry firewood, I catch fire. I start burning before Mama is ready. Question: How do I learn to simmer until Mama is ready? And what if Mama doesn't intend to cook immediately? Or she chooses to use the microwave?

"...I am looking at a lot of philosophical questions; what good is a road if it will ultimately not lead to happiness? Where did I come from? Who am I? What is the purpose of my life? What kind of person do I want to be? How should I live? What really matters? Do I want it to be said that I dreamt? Or that I achieved my dream? That I tried? Or that I accomplished?

"I am undergoing a critical search for meaning. I am trying to respond effectively to the forces of nature I face. I try to be principled without being an extremist, flexible without being brittle. I want to be resigned but not uninvolved. But most importantly, I want to love more than I want to be loved. There had been so many beginnings in my life with so few finishes. I feel like a failure when I know that I have not fulfilled the duty that comes with my privileges, especially when I feel it is divine in nature. The responsibilities that come with rights. But most importantly, I am fighting to face faith, my faith; and reason, my reason, equally. Finding the balance for these elements is the very ground of my battle.

"... I do not feel that the danger is that I am changing. Rather, it is that I am not. It would have been a sustainable situation if I was not being told that the only way for me to remain the same is to change... I have vowed to follow this story of you and I to the end. I will juggle my obsession, if that is what it is, with my thought. I will develop my images and hold on to my perceptions. I will maintain my attachments and solidify my clinging. To the world, I may be a one-person army fighting a cause of a lifetime. But there will be peace in my grave if once in a while you remember that I love you."

In other words, I will marry when I want.

Saving Mama Udoka

The two of us waited outside his office for over half an hour. She did not say a word to me despite three attempts on my part to start a conversation. Not even when I dropped the ultimate discussion generator: this country sucks. She looked timid in her flowery gown. The gown was sewn in an obsolete Nigerian fashion. She appeared to be in her early 20's and very weary of the American society. I could see that from the way she reacted when he walked out of his office to peek at those waiting for him. She quickly jumped out of her seat and sent out a loud "Good Morning, Sir." Looking at her, it was obvious she was very anxious. More than thrice, she adjusted her gown to make sure she looked good. Once she brought out a pocket mirror from her handbag and checked her face. With a trembling hand, she applied light make-up to spots she felt hadn't received adequate make up. Merely observing her gesture, it was apparent this meeting was very important to her.

I was there to find out from him how the Nigerian community was doing in his city. I was doing an informal study on love and marriage – the trends and travails. He is a well-respected community leader; the type people at home call "big man". He owns an employment agency that employs a lot of immigrant workers. Men and women searching for a start in the New World always accost him. His position gives him a pivotal insight into several issues affecting the lives of people. He does not just manage a business in the human services, but he also manages people. And that was why I chose him for this study.

She went in first to see him. Twenty minutes later, she walked out with a wide smile on her face, her anxiety all gone.

She waved goodbye and walked away quickly and happily.

When I went in to meet him, I asked him what he did that put a smile on the woman's face.

"I offered her a job," he answered.

"Why would a job be so important to her?" I asked.

"Because she has never worked in this country for all the three years she has been here. Her husband kept her at home and turned her into a baby-making machine. She has given birth to three kids in three years. She doesn't go anywhere with her husband and she doesn't participate in community activities. She just stays home with the babies. She does not drive, so she cannot go out alone. There is no reliable public transportation system where she lives, so she is more or less dependent on her husband who works at night and comes home tired. For three years, she has depended on her husband for everything. Now, her mother-in-law has come to live with them and she is stepping out for the very first time."

"The coming of her mother-in-law must be a great relief for her and her husband," I said.

"Not really. It is now the beginning of a new conflict. Her husband is threatening to send her and the children back to Nigeria if she defies him and goes out to get a job."

She was a college student at the University of Nigeria, Nsukka (UNN), when he came from America and asked her to marry him. She was 22 years old, while he was 38, though at that time, he told her he was 33 years. She wanted to come to America, even though she did not know why. All her beautiful young friends were marrying young men who lived abroad and she too wanted to marry one. The alternative she knew would have been to marry a trader, the idea of which she hated. She had resisted marrying other men from her ethnic group who were based in other foreign countries, and her parents had begun to panic. She had been told repeatedly how difficult it would be to find a husband after she graduated from the university. Her mother had warned her about many young girls who were coming of age and would soon steal the spotlight from her. "You see Aunt Ebele," her mother was fond of saying, "she used to be stunningly beautiful. She made *inyanga* for all the men who came to marry her. Now, see how miserable she is." All these stories scared her. She capitulated.

To say that her husband is insecure is an understatement. He firmly believed that if he let her step out, there were young men who would take her away from him. So he vowed to keep her away from public view. To keep her busy, he made sure she was pregnant almost all the time. To his friends who showed concern for her, he would remind them that he has been taking care of all her needs without complaints.

"When the kids are grown, then you will complete your education." That was his standard answer to her demand to finish college. Privately though, he would tell his friends that her schooling would only resume when she got older and less attractive. She yearned to understand the society she found herself in. She was eager to make her own money, no matter how little, and be able to assist her parents and siblings without having to beg. "You should be happy you have a husband who hasn't turned you into a money making machine. Haven't you heard of other men who specifically married nurses and brought them to the US to slave away? I provide you with all your needs and this is how you show your gratitude?" her husband would scold.

The first time he came to visit her at Zik's Flat hostel at UNN, she was rehearsing her lines for Shakespeare's *Romeo and Juliet*. She was Juliet in the school play. Four years later, she wondered how she seemed to have abandoned all her ideals, her vision of life, love and happiness. Her dream of a young Romeo who would love and cherish her had since been turned upside down. And even the 'bliss' of being in America, she could not lay claim to. She thought of her fall from a bubbling chickito to Mama Udoka and could not fathom what had happened to her. One morning, after a talk with her Nigerian neighbour in their dilapidated apartment, she decided to find herself a job.

Thirty minutes later, I stepped out of his office and found her by the bus stop waiting for Bus 261. I walked up to her and introduced myself. And she began to talk....

I am a girl trapped in a woman's body. My life is what some will call 'girl, interrupted'. When I was a teenager, I believed I had star qualities. I was exotic, sprightly and inviting. I envisaged myself being something more than just the woman next door. It was my dream to contribute to my society. I grew up playing up my best features and ignoring the worst. I modelled my life principles after my makeup regimen. I blurred and bled my makeup layers. I avoided strokes, swipes and straight lines. I used a little of the same blush; I gave drama to the eyes. I avoided black eyeliners and mascara. When I applied makeup, I did so in natural light.

His idea of fun on a weekday after work is to sit in front of the television with the remote control, channel surfing and on weekends lie on the couch all day long snoring. After the kids go to bed, he would watch *Girls Gone Wild* videos. For me, not being able to go to the theatre or see a movie, I would sit and read Dame Barbara Cartland romance novels. He hardly reads. I believe the last book he read (fiction or otherwise) was in college in the early '80s. He has this bookshelf at home filled with books on business and finance, knowledge he is yet to put to use; that is, if he ever acquired it. When he sees me reading, he feels threatened. "Don't get yourself worked up over things you read in books," he would say, "reality is very different from what the books say."

When he is done watching naked women flouncing around, he would come looking for sex by asking if I wanted some. I do not mind sex if only he would be romantic about it and a little adventurous. But what I get is the same boring thing night after night, year in and year out. He would not even make love in the morning or afternoon. It was always at night with the lights turned off. Woe betides me if I sought out sex from him. He did not think good Igbo women asked for sex. He also thought it very disrespectful for a wife to initiate any sexual contact. But, if there is anything I have learnt from all the years of sitting at home watching soap operas, Jerry Springer and Oprah, it is that talking about one's emotional anguish is the first step in healing. I have tried to get him to loosen up, but he is so set in his ways. When would he realize that there are other ways of making love besides the 'missionary style.' Things he loved for me to do for him and to him before we got married, all of a sudden are taboo in this house. Now when I do those things for him he says "only prostitutes do things like that." I feel so sexually frustrated. Love making in this house seems to be only for procreation.

As a young girl, I dreamt about marrying a man who would show me love. A man who would take me on long walks along narrow paths, hold my hands, caress me softly and rub my hair, lay with me on green grass, whisper sweet nothings into my ears, kiss me passionately under the full moon and make me his princess. I dreamt of being a valued member of my family, a voice in the decision making process. I had thought that my husband and I would be partners in life's long journey. Little did I know that I would be turned into 'that woman' or just 'Mama Udoka', whose only life function is to clean the house, take care of the kids, pick up after my husband and have sex when and how he feels like it. I waste away without being appreciated or respected. In short, I am just a doormat.

I love theatre. I love movies. But since I came to this country, I have not had the opportunity to explore any of these interests. He would not let me. He frustrates all my attempts to maintain friendship with other women my age. He claims they would spoil me. He would not even let me watch BET or listen to Hip-Hop music. He says Tupac, Destiny's Child, TLC, Ja Rule and other similar artistes promote decadent forms of entertainment. Mind you, this is the type of music I grew up on.

He listens to Marvin Gaye, the Cool and the Gang, Osadebe, Sir Warrior and other musicians of the '60s and '70s. We would fight in the car when I tuned the radio to more modern and contemporary channels. A break from his Osadebe cassette tapes would not be permitted.

Once in a while, I like to eat out, or order in. When I first came to the US, he took me out every other week. Now, like my sex life, that is a thing of the past. Even when I am ill, I still have to cook for the family, while he lies on his couch with his remote control. It is bad enough that I have to cook when I am ill, but he still has to make outrageous demands, like saying he would not eat any soup that is more than two days old, or that he would not eat rice kept in the fridge. I also want to try other kinds of food, like American dishes, Chinese food and even Thai and Indian food. But oh God, he is so fixated on his African dishes. When I prepare anything other than Nigerian food for the kids and I, he is quick to remind me that I am wasting money. "Where a poor girl like you picked up this sweet mouth, I do not know, and it is not like you are even bringing any money to this house," he would grumble.

I know there are many in our community who would say I am a bad woman when they hear me talk like this; that I am badmouthing my husband. But mine is a cry for help. My mother's generation was brought up with the notion that silence in the face of emotional abuse and unhappiness is a virtue. I owe it to myself and to my children's generation to begin the process of changing all of that and healing. I don't think my husband is necessarily a wicked or evil man and that he is doing all of this just to punish me. I think that our conflicts are a result of a generational gap and the way males are brought up in Nigeria. My decision for now is to put my foot down, do what I know is right and get him to take a whole new look at life.

People who have known him for a long time have told me he was not always like this. They said he was a kind gentleman when he first came to America. I tend to believe them for he is nothing like his parents, which is a story for another day. I was told that his first wife whom he married in order to get his green card really dealt with him. She literally made him use his toothbrush to clean the toilet, I hear. On a daily basis, the two of them fought themselves to a standstill, but he put up with her for fear of not getting his green card. The six years they were together totally transformed him, a classmate of his revealed. Now, he is a shadow of his former self—drained—emotionally and psychologically. He is absolutely afraid of anything that reminds him of her.

Yet, I do not think I should let myself be a punching bag for whatever flashback he is experiencing. I, too, have my life to live. The sins of another woman should not be visited on me. I have tried to be as different from his first wife as possible in order to make him feel secure and comfortable. I have even given up wearing any decent clothing. He calls them provocative dressing and unfit for a married woman. Even the negligees I wear just for him are evidence of low moral standards. One summer day, on the anniversary of our wedding, I wore a strapless dress and he freaked out. He ordered me to remove the dress. I resisted. That was the first of many times that he hit me. Previously I would just sit there and cry. These days, I hit back.

Over the weekend, as I push my Stop and Shop carriage filled with dirty laundry in a black trash bag to the local Laundromat, I hear a car horn. I take a quick glance from the corner of my eyes and quickly see a rather handsome black guy in the car. He looks vaguely familiar, but I don't stare or stop to speak with him for fear either my husband or one of his friends would see me. My heart is thumping and I cringe at the thought that perhaps this guy knew me in Nigeria in my 'babe days'. To think that anybody who knew me from my University days would see me pushing a shop cart with Udoka sitting in the carriage, his nose dripping with mucus sliding towards his mouth and both hands stuffed with fried plantains, I cringed.

As soon as I start working, I will pay for driving lessons and get my driver's license. No need asking him to teach me how to drive for that would be like knocking on the horn of a toad. When I earn a little money, I will buy myself a used car. Only then will I be truly free in this land of the free and the home of the brave. In the meantime, I will continue to sit here and wait for Bus 261.

Just Before You Kill Your Wife

There are so many reasons to kill your wife, a wife, any wife. I knew this even before I got married. So I am not going to debate that with you after five years of marriage.

If I want, I can call you stupid – stupid for ignoring that warning written on the gwomgworo 911 lorry, plying the Onitsha-Nsukka road that says, "Fear Women." You did not fear women. You stubbornly went ahead and got married. I wanted to say, "*Ntoo,*" but I didn't because what I intend to say here is serious, and I do not want to lose you.

So let's jump to the reasons why you may need to kill your wife.

She makes more money than you do. Okay, it's not really the higher earning power that pisses you off, it is the spending. She does not hand the paycheque to you so you can decide what it should be spent on. Okay, I know. You don't really want her to hand the money over to you, you are not that kind of bushman. In fact, you don't even care what she spends it on. You just don't want her to demean you in the manner that she spends the money. Yes, like putting up a storeyed building in her father's compound when your parents still live in a mud house. After all, you brought her to America and paid her school tuition as well as the mortgage while she studied nursing. You did that by driving a taxi. You deserve more respect.

Ha, she came from a well-to-do family. Yes, the elite high society family. You got to marry her because you live in

America. America nullifies status and allows you to cross the social line. You lied to her about what you were doing in America. But you have since resolved that. You thought she only married you just to come to America, but you have had three kids and you have forgotten about that fear. You have begun real estate agent classes, so you will soon be wearing suit and tie. But now, her family is telling her what to do. She is listening to them. They are treating you like trash. Yes, especially that evil mother-in-law. They won't back off from your marriage. Everyone is still mocking you. You brought her to America, and this is the thanks that you get.

You did not tell me, but I heard it through the wide-open grapevine. She is following other men. She did not tell you that you were not satisfying her in bed or that you are too old for her. But she is following younger men, some half your age. No, it wasn't the *akata* men that made you mad; it was other Nigerian men who now tell everyone that your wife is "Mrs Donatus." It breaks your heart and makes you feel impotent when you know you are not. You have even gone out of your way to buy books and films just to help improve your sex life. But it looks like it is too little too late. It doesn't seem like she will come back to you.

Didn't I hear you say that she isn't beautiful anymore? You said you needed to find younger women to make you feel young again. But being as stubborn as she is, she won't let you be. She keeps following you around, threatening to divorce you and take you to the cleaners. You have said to her that if it were in Africa, you would have married an additional three wives. I hear you. You need to do something to stop her. The nagging, the fighting, and the threat to half of all you worked very hard for. I hear you. The insurance business you have been building for the last twenty years.

I heard that the judge awarded her $3000 in child support money every month. He also gave her and the kids your home. Add that to the $3000 she makes in a month and you will see why she has so much money that she throws around with one boyfriend after another. Meanwhile, you make $4000 a month and after paying her the money that she squanders, you are left with $1000. It is not enough to pay the rent in your small apartment. Not enough to begin your life again. Now, she doesn't even want you to have visitation rights. She lies to the judge that you are a threat to your own children, just like she lied that you make more money than you actually do. It is provocative. I know.

She said she went to university in Nigeria. You brought her here and had hoped to send her to nursing school. She could not pass even the CNA class. She has failed nursing entrance examination four times. She is so dumb that you often think she needs help crossing the road. She is good at watching TV. That's it. She won't even keep the house clean.

She is a liability you need to get rid of as safely as possible.

There are many reasons to kill your wife, a wife, any wife. I bet you can come up with more and more.

For now, I want to tell you about an armed robber I admired so much. He was 63 years old. He walked into a bank and gave the teller a note saying that he was robbing the bank. The teller gave him all the money she had on her station and pressed the red button. The man walked out of the door and handed the money to the bank's security guard. He waited for the police. They came and arrested him. Upon investigation, it was discovered that earlier the man had given out all his valuables and had returned his apartment key to his landlord, telling him he would not be coming back. When asked why he did what he had done, the robber said he could only get minimum wage jobs and was tired of living hand-to mouth. He said he felt it would be better to spend two years in prison, with free food and free medical care and by the time he is out, he is qualified to collect social security benefit.

That is the robber after my heart.

Just before you kill your wife, decide on where you will wait for the police. I don't want to hear that you ran into the bush or took off in a car with your kids. You embarrass me by that kind of action. You know they will catch you so why don't you do the honourable thing and act like you are ready for them.

So before you kill your wife, pay off what you owe the Igbo organization of your city, including the one for the Igbo House Project so that if you die in prison they may send your body home, which is necessary for you to reincarnate. Oh, never mind. For a moment, I forgot that those who committed *alu*, abomination, do not reincarnate.

Just before you kill your wife, return that Nigerian movie you borrowed from me. You don't have to pay off your credit cards, or car payment, but at least, settle the pepper soup woman at our joint. She needs that money to continue to serve our community while you are cooling off in prison.

Just before you kill your wife, remember that it will become official that O. J. Simpson is a descendant of the Igbo if another Igbo man kills his wife in America.

Just before you kill your wife, picture your children coming to the gate of that state penitentiary to pick you up after you have served 30 years. Imagine how you will feel when they open the door of that Limo and let you in. And I hope you will smile wildly when they take a selfie with you and say, "Dad, thank you for killing Mom."

Just before you kill your wife, remember your father had many good reasons to kill your mother. But he didn't.

Hopefully, you are thankful for that.

This American Life Sef!

You come to America, young and dashing, on a full scholarship, finish school, get a great job, marry a glamorous spouse, have cute children, and retire at a young age with a great pension, portfolio and posture.

...And live happily ever after. Yes champ; rub it in. For the rest of you, life abroad is a crest of trajectories.

You come into America, by air, by sea, or via a midnight sneak-in across the Mexican border; fooling the Minute Men and Lou Dobbs all at once. You come to school, to join your spouse, to work after winning the Green Card Lottery, or to raise your hand at the airport and claim persecution in your own country because you are a Mormon as well as a leader in MEND.

You behold America the beautiful. The triple-decker burgers and the giant cup of coke and cars that are wider than your village road and you wonder what took you so long to get here. You get on with schooling. For now any cheap school will do. You study the things people who came before you say brings money – the things Americans do not want to study- to prepare you for the job Americans do not want to do. You hear nursing, bloody, nursing. You say, bring it on. You get on with marriage - convenience marriage- discovering that you married three persons at once; the person you thought you married, the person your spouse really is and the person your spouse becomes because you got married in this America. For work, you do anything for a dollar; cut meat in fast food restaurants, drive a cab, guard the parking lot of company executives younger than you, even care for the disabled, breaking your back to pay the bills.

Then reality hits. The dollar is not adding up. There's more going out than there is coming in. Time is running. Letters, emails and phone calls are enveloping you from home. School is done; where is the job? Your accent is a problem. Racism is real. You're finally squeezed in. Then comes a Corporate job at last. Work place politics really sucks. Meanwhile, the American spouse is gone but your residency is established. Now where do you find someone to marry for real? A blind date? E-harmony.com? Town conventions? What of picking up someone from your village? But these are all packages which content you cannot ascertain. Somehow, you settle with one. Honeymoon over, now what is the state of the marriage? First mission accomplished, now what next?

You start a house in your village. A big house. You sink in any money you can get. Some of it goes to the building of the house but most of it goes to your family member who is supervising the construction. It costs more than it would to buy a comparable house in America. You are afraid to calculate how many days you will sleep in this house in your lifetime. You say, *Tufiakwa*. It will not be your portion. You need to do it not just because everyone is doing it – your daddy is demanding it. He's asking you to wipe away the shame on the family's face.

Your daddy dies. Your dentist extracts a tooth.

Then America begins to reveal itself quietly. Oh tribalism again; discrimination at the workplace. Your head touches the virtual ceiling for immigrants. You now understand affirmative action. Kids come, but housemaids are tagged slavery, who will care for them? Now you have day care, mortgage, after school sport activities, mid-life career crisis, more phone calls from home, and marital problems. If only some of these can wait. You can call marital problems by its real name- money problems entangled with control problems, decision-making disagreements, tasks and privileges, status problems and in-law problems. Maybe you will stay home with the kids. Maybe your mother will come and help ... and incense your spouse.

With caning banished, you raise teens with your hands tied to your back. Marital problems persist because as your fortune falls, that of your spouse rises. You have done your calculation. Something has to give. You try selling real estate. You prepare taxes. You sell insurance. You run out of contacts. You buy cars from the auction and ship them home. You get duped by friends and family. Nothing is adding up.

Fast insurance fraud deals? You try other businesses on the side, but total dedication is needed. You quit your job entirely and start a business. Cleaning business. Staffing business. Medical equipment. Home Health business. Escort service. Oh, these taxes, running costs, government paperwork and lack of patronage by your own people.

Marital problems persist. You wish you had married the lover you left in Nigeria to come to America. You take the divorce option. Half of your wealth is wiped out in the process. Now rages the battle for visitation rights, alimony and child support. You're estranged from the kids because of the stories your spouse made up against you to win custody. But you keep paying up. You have no option. You start afresh. A new apartment. Maybe a new spouse? No, that can wait. Your classmate at home becomes the CEO of a multinational company. A chieftaincy title follows and you wonder what happened to you.

You consider a fast 419 advance fee fraud deal. You remember those acquaintances still doing time in US prisons. You hold off. You dream of a contract from the government at home. You write a proposal. You get in touch with an old classmate who has done well.

Home looks attractive. The people you left behind are doing better. You conveniently forget the majority who are not making ends meet. You are overwhelmed. High blood pressure is diagnosed. High cholesterol. Heart problems. Another tooth is extracted. You join the gym. You stay away from garri and Farina. You join a church. You can be a pastor too, but you don't like that lifestyle of pretending to be what you're not. Life is no more fun. You go home, dabble in business, in politics, in entertainment.

You are burnt. You return. You start afresh.

No, you won't take the divorce option. You will manage. You will live like roommates, until the kids are grown and are out of the house. You will wait for retirement. You need just ten more years. At 56, with social security plus pension pay and 401K, you can go to the village, if kidnappers permit, and enjoy your old age. And start afresh. Maybe marry anew. Maybe teach in a college in Nigeria. Yeah! You register for a PhD with an online college.

Your Mummy dies. Your dentist extracts another tooth. Your doctor suggests knee and hip replacement. Your shrink prescribes Prozac.

In spite of your *wahala*, the children grow. The girls do well in school. The boys go from four-year colleges to two- year colleges, in-between gang membership and police troubles. The boys marry White girls. The girls marry African American guys. You're glad the girls did not get pregnant out of wedlock. You thank God the boys did not throw a coming out party to announce that they are gay. One lives in Arizona and another in Hawaii. Your house is empty, calls come on holidays only.

It is now time to really go home. But what about managing the diabetes? Do you trust the doctors at home to handle your dialysis? Your medication cocktail will be hard to find at home. Daddy and Mummy are dead. You have to make new friends again. The ones you used to have are now strangers to you. Your spouse refuses to go with you. Spouse cannot deal with the sound of electric generators, untreated well water, *Afor Igwe* meat without an FDA inspection tag.

You retire. You sell the big house and move into a small condo. When you cannot wipe your behind, you go from the condo to a nursing home. Your children are too busy to have you share their homes. They visit every presidential election year. Once again, you think of going home but no, it is rather too late for that. The twelfth tooth is gone. You now take more pills than the teeth in your mouth.

So you stay until your autopsy is ready. Your townsfolk contribute money to ship you home. As your coffin lands in Lagos, your relations who have gathered to receive you for the last time mutter in-between breaths, *Tufiakwa*. Yes, the same *Tufiakwa* that you said the time you read the article called 'This American Life'.

Oh, about your kids, well, some of them went home with your body. Those few times you cleaned your bank account to take them home paid off. They watch as sand lands on your coffin. One even remembered how to say, '*Kedu*'. They leave soon after. They will come back one more time – when they accompany your ex on the final journey home.

Our Children Are Coming

Contrary to what many Nigerians at home think, living abroad has numerous downsides. Many who migrated abroad find out after a while that they do not belong to either the society they left at home or the new one they inhabit abroad. Aside from all the problems associated with surviving in a foreign land, those abroad miss a valuable opportunity to grow up with their extended family and friends they made in the early stages of life. Often, some simple pleasures of life, usually underestimated, come together later in the course of our adventure abroad to make life awful, if not miserable. I have heard an elderly Nigerian complain that his greatest loss was his inability to marry his high school sweetheart as a result of his decision to emigrate. By all accounts, the most frightening downside of living abroad is the possibility of losing our children to the new society.

The Nigerian child born abroad is at best a hyphenated Nigerian. More often than not, these kids are not Nigerians in both nature and nurture. The forces of the society they were born into usually frustrate every attempt by parents to raise them up as Nigerians. As these children grow, parents are at a loss as to how to imbibe in them the things they had while at the same time giving them the things they did not have. It is the greatest dilemma of life abroad.

What has been proven beyond reasonable doubt is that, no matter how much parents tried, Nigerian children born abroad who had no chance of forming a strong attachment to Nigeria are most likely to see their host country as their home. This leaves most parents in an unpleasant position where they face the possibility of spending their retirement years alone in Nigeria or in a nursing home abroad. It is one prospect no Nigerian parent wants.

Many parents are currently trying various approaches to the problem with little success. There seem to be a consensus that the only way to make the children born abroad develop an attachment to their parents' home country is to have them live for a while at home or visit often. When to visit home and how long to visit is still not clear. When to send the children home and for how long hasn't been ironed out.

The logistics of sending a child home are enormous. There is the question of who will take care of the child at home? There is the anxiety over insecurity at home and lack of basic healthcare facilities. But more importantly, there are questions about the very nature of the knowledge today's Nigeria will be able to impart on these kids. No doubt, the Nigeria of today is a far cry from two decades ago. How much of what rubs off today's Nigerian youths do parents want their kids to pick up? Are the admired values acquired by these parents few decades ago still obtainable in Nigeria?

Currently, a good number of parents send their children to Nigeria for their high school education. The reasoning behind this is that it is manageable at that age. Most parents cannot emotionally afford to send a toddler home even when they have reliable relations. And by the time a kid has finished high school abroad, it is much more difficult to get their cooperation. Also with persistent strikes and closures, college education in Nigeria has become unappealing.

There are other formulas being tried out. In some cases, one of the parents opts to go home to raise the kids. This could only work in few cases where the financial and marital health of the couple is strong. There are cases where regular visits to Nigeria for holidays is the approach being adopted. But again, very few people can afford this. Some parents in big cities try to create a home away from home. They establish networks in which Nigerian children relate with one another and in some cases attend language classes, seeking means to encourage courtships leading to marriage.

Despite all these efforts, the success rate of children born abroad identifying with the home country of their parents is relatively low. They seem to be overpowered by the pressures of their host country's mainstream culture. The most likely direction of these children is the adoption of the lifestyle of their peers in an effort to belong. This often ranges from minor irritations like tongue piercing to major concerns like interracial marriages. What follows are decisions that greatly reduce the chances of the child ever returning to Nigeria. Which means that most Nigerian parents abroad would either retire in a nursing home abroad or alone at home. That is one unpalatable possibility that stares many Nigerian parents in the face.

A look beyond the first generation born abroad presents a bleaker picture. For even in those rare cases where the parents succeeded, there is an even slimmer chance that the second generation of Nigerians born abroad would succeed in stopping their children from completely assimilating into the new society.

What this means, then, is that Nigerian parents abroad are basically fighting a losing battle. One hundred years from now, their lineage at home would be forgotten entirely. Their epitaph would read like those sold into slavery 400 years ago. The big houses some are currently building in cities and villages across Nigeria would be taken over by relatives left at home. Many who are already seeing this possibility and cannot live with it are beginning to regret the very day they went to the foreign embassy to seek a visa. Some, though very few, have returned home to face whatever challenge they encounter at home.

In a recent discussion of this issue with my friend, Obinna, he came up with a classic macho plan to resolve the problem.

His plan is to marry one wife in America and another in Nigeria. When he is ready to go home and retire, he would have a family at home to spend his twilight years with. Next week, I will visit Obinna and essentially discuss his plan with his girlfriend, Ify. I can't wait to hear what she thinks of Obinna's plan.

This American Life Sef! II.

You survived. You are one of the few who did. By survival I mean, you have spent 15, 20, 30 or more years in America without jumping bail, going to jail, getting deported or getting killed.

You know many who did well for themselves, people who got education and started a profession as a lawyer, doctor, engineer, pharmacist, nurse, realtor, etc. They took it a notch up. They started something of their own. They worked hard, only for them to hit what they call a wall of misfortune, loss of professional license for acts unbecoming of their profession, allegation of fraud, expensive trial, huge fine, confiscation of property, jail time.

Granted, you have diabetes, high blood pressure and high cholesterol. You are considered a chronic patient, which means that, other than your friends and colleagues, your doctors will not be surprised if anything happens to you at any time. The doctors already have a choice of dozens of diseases to blame. As far as they are concerned, you have pre-existing conditions that could lead to a heart attack, stroke, heart failure, renal failure, or ultimately, death.

You survived. Your children have grown. They are in the universities. They have graduated. You see them moving on with their lives with little help from you. In fact, you now have to cajole them to come home on holidays. They prefer to be on their own, independent of you. Your new worry is about the person they should marry. You hope it is someone from where you came from. But the friends you see them with does not give you much hope. It keeps you awake at night.

Your marriage survived. You went through those rough patches when most of the marriages of Africans in America collapse. That was when both of you put legs in one trouser because you felt you could do better, that you still had great prospects. Now you have adjusted to each other. One of you picks up the socks and, in exchange, the other makes okra soup. Or one of you is tired of nagging about little things like the socks and sundry matters and have practically moved into one of the other rooms your children vacated. In fact, that thing they say about old couples is happening to you. People are beginning to say that you look alike, like brother and sister, except that one appears to have bleached; you bleached your face and shoulders and forgot your hands and legs.

Okay, your marriage did not survive. But you have adjusted well to the custody battle, child support, shared custody, second partner and the multiple families. Or you have carried on well as a single fellow. You cannot stand going through the marriage thing again. You get by with others like you. It is the American way. You sigh at the mention of "till death do us part." You are an authority on how America changes African people in marriage situations. You can write a book on that.

You survived. With the kids virtually on their own you suddenly found out that you have more leisure time. No more fighting with the boys to stay away from video games and concentrate on their school work. No more school runs to drop off or pick up kids. No more birthday parties, soccer games, piano lessons or basketball games. They drive themselves now to places they want to go. You just sit at home and worry about their driving. You hold your breath each time they hit the road, wondering if they will text while they drive. You also worry about how much their car insurance has added to your family car insurance bill. You cannot wait for them to turn 26 and get their own car insurance.

You have figured out how to use your new found free time. You will join one or more of those African associations, organizations and clubs. Those groups that you ignored when you were busy raising your kids and advancing your career. They are becoming attractive to you. Not just as a social group where you go to reminisce about the good old days, but also people who may help take your body home when the time arrives. You have looked at your children and you are not sure if they care enough about what happens to you when the final call comes.

You join sons of this, daughters of that club. You form Elite club of this city and Elite club of that city. You join the People's Club. The club whose theme song says, "Let's enjoy life, afterward we'll figure out tomorrow." You were not attracted to flamboyant display of wealth and loud lifestyle, but something has changed in you. Now you don't mind being called chief of something; after all, Americans have Fire Chief, Chief of Surgery and Chief Justice. In fact, you are contemplating getting one of those traditional titles they give out at home for the right price. It is either that or you go for one of those titles that the churches are dishing out for a fee—elder, deacon, knight, minister. Anything to stand out in public and fill in the emptiness that life in America has become.

You are yet to figure out tomorrow. But you are on it. After putting in 15 - 25 years at work, you are ripe for retirement with full pension. You see that if you retire now you can live on your pension before social security kicks in. You can even start something on the side—export business, driving Uber, starting an NGO, anything to keep you busy and earn an extra quid.

You survived. Your doctors now try every new medication in the market on you. In the morning, even before you say your prayers to God, you say one to the pharmaceutical industry, visit your pillbox and count out the morning pills. Over the years, you have noticed that the pills you ingest before or after each meal keep increasing in numbers, shapes and colours. The doctors hardly remove old ones before they add new ones. You don't need anyone to tell you that time is ticking.

So you get irritated when someone suggests that you control what you eat. You retort, "we proceed to the great beyond with what we ate." With all these your people in medical fields, everywhere you go you hear them say you should exercise — take a walk, run, join the gym. You are paying for gym membership but you hardly go near the place. To your credit, you try to take a walk every now and then. But your knee is beginning to ache. Your doctor once said you may need knee replacement down the road. You don't even want to revisit that discussion with him. It was enough that he talked and talked and talked until you went for a colonoscopy.

At social gatherings, you try to dance the diseases away. You do shoki, Azonto, Alingo, Makossa, Suokous and galala. People around do not understand the spiritual angle to your jives. You don't blame them. They don't know what it is like to carry insulin around in a bag.

You survived. And because you did, you are seriously thinking about retiring and going back home. Your pension and social security check will carry you through. That means you have to go and chase out the lizards occupying that mansion you built in the village years ago that you have never spent up to 100 days in. That mansion that took a large chunk of your 401K, retirement money that you borrowed at great penalty. Oh, haven't you completed the mansion? Thinking of retirement means that you have to finish that mansion. Since your folks at home have ripped you off in the name of getting the work done for you, you decide to go home and complete the job yourself.

As days go by and arthritis and rheumatism invade, the prospect of retiring in Africa intrigues you the more. To get ready, you register at the University of Phoenix or any of the other online universities that promises to give you a PhD with or without a dissertation. You will need their online PhD to fit in at home where titles and degrees are the great social divider.

You have worked out how to get your supply of mediations at home. Your social security check is guaranteed to arrive each month. You have imagined each morning grabbing the fresh palm wine from the village tapper before he adds sugar and water to the keg. As for who would be rubbing your back at night during harmattan season, you will work that out when you get home.

You have your plans worked out and then, your doctor calls…

This American life sef!

Short Stories

A Kernel for a Fowl

After years of pursuing men, you believed in a man being dropped right into your arms. It was the Almighty's purpose for you. And that was how you met him. It validated your belief. It hardened your heart to everything else anyone was saying, including Ihuoma, your girlfriend. From then on, everything else was undue mocking of tired people. And coming from Ihuoma, who had not fared any better in the hands of men, you had no problem waving it aside. You had no fear that, like she said, you might be cracking a kernel for a fowl.

You were a nurse, a degree-holding Registered Nurse. You never forgot that you ought to be rich. You worked round the clock. Every shift American nurses declined, you would accept. Holidays and all, you were available. In fact, you loved the holidays because you got paid double the time. And at sixty dollars an hour, a double meant more than a new hairstyle. It meant a day at the spas, a visit to Bloomingdale's and another bottle of Agent Provocateur.

You drove a big BMW, an SUV model. Most men who had the opportunity to get close were intimidated by your confidence and poise. Those who were not, who dared to approach you with brilliant Pick-up lines, you had doubts about their sincerity. You could not figure out if they were coming to you because of your hard earned money or to take advantage of the residency status which you had earned as a nurse.

It wasn't long ago when he told you that you belonged to him. You assumed that it meant he belonged to you. You were an African, but you now you live in America. You cook with the microwave and you bathe in the bathtub. You fetch no firewood and you draw no well water. You eat hamburgers and not *foofoo*. You wear jeans and not a *buba*. No proverbs were created around computers, iPods and GPS systems, so you accepted that it meant all proverbs were suspended. You had crossed seven seas and seven rivers. You had left behind the seven idioms of the seven shrines of your homeland. You were now in the land of the free and the home of the brave.

All old things had passed away.

So you allowed him to etch a tattoo down your waistline. He tattooed you that first night he made love to you. You let him draw a big stop sign. He painted it red, too. When you wore a tank top, the red sign showed at your waistline. Your panties often split the sign into two. Further down, he wrote a special note. He ended it with an exclamation mark. His note read: Private property – do not trespass. Scorpions on guard, ready to sting objects as little as index fingers - men beware! Then you lay there for three hours as he drew a scorpion. You did not mind as he scraped off some pubic hair to find space for its tail.

He asked you to tattoo him too. But you were no tattoo artist. You were just a nurse. You told him not to worry. You did not need to draw your face around his penis to be assured of his faithfulness. When he asked you what you would have drawn, you lied to him. You did not tell him you would have drawn a long rose stem. Instead, you said to him, "I would have drawn a gun and simply written beside it, in capital letters, BANG." You knew you were lying. But lying had become part of your life. Your true self had not taken you anywhere.

You were not always like this. In fact, when you came to America, you carried with you, like a little shell, all the norms you learnt at home. You dared not look a man deep in the eyes. Your Mama taught you to carry yourself with grace. Growing up in Enugu, you were able to resist the pressures of your peers.

You still hear your mother's voice. "Uzo, don't be like those loose girls who are spoilt and are not good for marriage." But her voice became fainter as each day passed. You had managed to confine her voice to a small cubicle where you stash things of the past.

If only Mama could see you, she would not believe what you had become. You had become a grown woman. A woman, ten times the woman she was. You knew what you wanted and how to get it. You did things that she could not imagine in this life and maybe, in the life to come. Somehow, you had learnt to please yourself. Sometimes you worry that you might be in a rush to recover the years you spent trying to please Mama. You do not regret those years. Without the restrictions, you probably would not have won the scholarship that brought you to America. But you were happy to throw away all inhibitions of the past.

He was the one who opened your eyes. He was the one who led you to places you did not know existed. In moments of bliss, you did not fail to remind him that he spoilt you. You liked to be spoilt. You liked to be pampered. You liked to be worshipped. You liked your man to think of nothing else but you. And you had succeeded with him. Like a tortoise, you had made him desire you. He desired you so much that he had agreed to lift the earth onto your head. Your only challenge was finding a place for him to stand as he did that.

You were not just a taker, you were also a giver. And that was how you met him. You were doing a graveyard shift at the trauma centre of Union Hospital in Lynn, Massachusetts, when paramedics rushed him into the hospital. A Latino gang member shot him right inside his barbershop/tattoo parlour. You were assigned to him after surgery to remove a bullet lodged in his thigh. A foot higher, the bullet would have shattered his manhood. When he came out of surgery, it was the first thing he said to you. And you laughed.

You cared for him that night. You cared for him like he was your brother. You continued to care for him in the days that followed. He had nobody around. His two brothers and sister all lived in London. You knew this because you bought the phone card and dialled the numbers for him as he informed them of his ordeal. They called. They sent him flowers. But they were too busy to fly to America. His parents in Nigeria were too busy with local politics to come too. His friends came when time permitted. But you were the one who was always there.

When he was discharged, you continued to visit him at home. You cooked and baked. You made meals, soups, and porridge. You helped him clean his house. You dressed his wound. You even helped him run his barbershop before he finally sold it. The gunshot he said, was just a warning. But for you, it was a sign you had wanted to see for so long. At first, you did not know why you were doing those things. But you were sure they were the right things to do.

It had been a while since you last did something because it was right. You had learned that, in America, because it was right wasn't a good reason to do anything. In America, experience had shown you, people did things mainly because it felt good. You had paid a heavy price before you learnt this. The scars on your soul, the patches on your emotions and the wrinkles in your smiles were constant reminders.

Caring for him felt good. Considering where you came from and what you had been through, it did not make sense. But deep inside your heart, it felt good. That was how it started and blossomed into a love affair.

Everything was going well until his mother came to visit. It was his mother who unmasked you. She was the one who told him who you really were; that poor *wawa* girl whose mother sold bean balls, *akara*, in front of Chief Obiozo's house. Yes, it was you.

His father and Chief Obiozo were friends, thus he was a friend of Chief Obiozo's children. He visited Chief Obiozo's house many times. You were a secondary school student then, some seventeen years ago, and so was he. You admired him. From the boys' quarters where you and your mother lived, you saw him drive in several times with Obiozo's children. You were jealous when you saw beautiful girls in his arms. You wished you were one of those girls.

When they threw parties, you peeped through your little window and wondered how great their lives were. But you remembered what Mama told you; that you were given a different destiny—whatever that meant. You knew that your place was lower than his, even though you were in the same class, but different schools. He was attending the elite College of Immaculate Conception, Enugu, while you were at the lowly Idaw River Girls Secondary School off Agbani Road, also in Enugu. In spite of your different stations in life, you knew about boundless goodness that surpassed all imaginations. You knew this because your father, a driver for Chief Obiozo, died during the Biafran war. He was Chief Obiozo's aide de camp. You were told he gave his life for Chief Obiozo to live. Faced with a bleak future, Chief Obiozo took you and your Mama into his house. He contributed to your education and you were almost like his daughter.

"Almost," you would say, because you were not part of Chief Obiozo's children's parties. You were not friends with their friends. If you were, you would have been in his life before now. When Chief Obiozo was not home, you were more of his children's servant than their friend. You remembered one night, during one of the wild parties Chief Obiozo's children threw, when Kenny, Obiozo's first child, called you in to perform a chore. You could not remember what the chore was. But you remembered going into the kids' wing of the big house and seeing a living room full of beer bottles and cigarette butts. Half-naked girls were lying on the carpet. You remembered seeing him there. You remembered him because he came to your rescue when one of Obiozo's children grabbed you and started fondling your breasts. You did not like what he said that night. You did not forget it, either. But you were still grateful that he rescued you. In fact, you have rationalized what he said so much that you have convinced yourself that he only said it to protect you.

"Leave that *ngbeke* alone," he said. It had the same effect on you then that "leave that nigger alone" would have had on you today. Only that now, you knew you would be grateful to a white man if he said that and saved you from possible rape in the hands of another white man. That was how you rationalized it and compartmentalized it. You packaged it and keep it where you store things of the past.

Then, his mother came and revealed them all.

You were kind to his mother, too. When she came, you took time off from work. You drove her around and showed her places. You shopped for her; bought her expensive jewellery and clothes. You took her to every mall and every outlet in New England. She only needed to look at an item twice before you picked it up for her. You took her to the museum. You took her to Faneuil Hall and New England Aquarium. At Boston Wang Theatre, you saw the Broadway show, Les Miserable. You rode on the Boston Duck Tour. You saw her laugh as the duck became a boat in the river and a bus on land. She marvelled at that. She called it an American wonder. You were glad she liked it because she did not like Salem, the Witch city. You gave her a good time.

You thought things went well. When she was leaving, you gave her money too. You were not trying to bribe her. You were not even acknowledging that the path to a man's surname often started with the approval of his mother. You were doing it because, on so many levels, it felt right.

She seemed grateful for all you did for her. After each outing, she gave you a little more crayfish. Then she gave you garri. By the time she gave you *ogiri*, you were sure you firmly had her in your camp. Not that it was your goal all the while. As you accompanied him to the airport to drop her off, she surprised you when she gave you some yards of lace and material for a wrapper. Even though it was the cheap *aba naanya* material, you were very grateful. As you hugged her for the last time, you called her Mama. It wasn't the first time you called her Mama, but this time, it came out with a deeper meaning.

By the time his mother visited, you had known him for over two years. You had seen him grow from nigger-wannabe to a well-balanced black man. It started with the gunshot wound but you had a lot to do with the final outcome. When he owned the barbershop, he also drove a cab. The two occupations placed him in direct contact with the most violent people in the society. You helped him in his transition. You bought him the equipment he needed to become a DJ. It was what he wanted. He did that for a little while but business was not booming. He abandoned that too.

You encouraged him to go into nursing. He resisted many times. He was afraid of math and he hated biology. You made him take the North Shore Community College LPN entrance examination. He failed thrice.

He said he wanted to be a computer network administrator. You paid five thousand dollars for him to attend a training institute. He completed his courses. He studied hard and obtained his A+ certification. By the time he was done, the computer boom had fizzled out. Those who were surviving were those who got in not for the money but for the love of computers. He got in for the money and when the money was not coming, he put away his chips.

Finally, he settled into real estate. He became a realtor. He wore a suit and tie, expensive shoes and went about seeking people who want to buy houses. He was good at it. He had a sweet mouth. And it helped that he was handsome. It made wives encourage their husbands to listen. Many listened and he sold many houses. You agreed with him that he had found his calling.

But then, all his friends and acquaintances who had good credit and could afford the down payments had all bought houses. His options began to narrow. You helped him buy two houses. It was a small business of renting for him. A cushion. You also helped him start a staff recruiting agency that sent nurses and direct support staff to nursing homes and group homes. For a long while, you and your nurse friends were his core base of nurses.

As you helped move him towards more stable and responsible career choices, you also noticed his stabilization. It was gradual. He reduced the number of days he went to the gym and began to see himself beyond the puffiness of his muscles. You noticed the changes from the nature of the haircuts he was getting. You could also see from the size of the pants he wore. As he slid from the hard-core hip-hop worldview to a middle class black outlook, the size of his pants reduced. His pants also climbed up his butt. You were glad that your man was coming home. You were hopeful that he was settling.

But as soon as his mother left, you noticed a change in him. He wasn't as open as before. You asked him once what was eating him and he said he was being pressured by his mother to get married. You tried to console him. You tried to tell him all parents were designed to think like that. You tried to tell him that your mother had also been pushing you in the same direction.

You did not tell him, "Hello? What's the problem?" You did not say, "I'm here!" No. You encouraged him to listen to his mother and yet to make his own decision.

When he suddenly announced that he was going home and would stay for two months, you did not have any worries. After all, it had been a long time since he was home. You volunteered to help him run his businesses, but he refused. That surprised you because you had been helping him in the past. But you did not read too much into it. Not even when his agency stopped calling you for work. You did not care because you were never short of work hours anyhow.

He went to Nigeria and called you once. You did not hear from him again. One month, two months, three months. You were worried. You sent him an email but he did not respond. You visited his house and there was no sign that he had come back. You visited his staffing agency office. It had been closed. You made enquiries. You spoke to his friends but nobody seemed to know anything.

Even though you missed him so much, you gave him his space. It was very painful as your birthday came. Last year, you travelled with him to Disney World. It was there that you marked your thirty-fourth birthday and he celebrated his thirty-sixth, which was two months after yours. You missed him but you also knew in your heart that he was God's gift to you. *Agaracha*, wanderer, you told yourself, must come back.

Then four months after he went away, during your birthday party, someone gave you a strange gift. It was an envelope with a business card inside. You looked at the business card. It was his. It showed his name, new address and phone number in Worcester. A note on the back of the card said he had returned from Nigeria with a nineteen-year old wife and they both live in Worcester.

You stormed out of your own party like buttocks stung by a vicious ant. You entered your car and drove to Worcester. You could not recall stopping at any traffic light. You could not remember paying any toll at Tobin Bridge. The last time you were in Worcester, you had come with him to attend a pre-wedding party of a Kenyan friend at Lucky Dog nightclub.

You got to the address and saw his Mercedes car parked in the driveway—a car you made the down payment for. You sat outside his house and watched, while your blood boiled inside. From the window you could see two figures moving around the house. You called the home number on the card. You saw him walk towards what must be the phone. He paused at what must be the phone's caller ID. He did not pick it up. You waited for two minutes. You called his new cell phone number. He did not pick that up either.

You sat in the car for a long time with your eyes focused on the house. As tears began to build up, you saw the two figures inside what looked like the living room area. He held her hand and they began to dance. The scene broke goose pimples all over your skin. You called again, this time dialling * 87 first to conceal your phone number. He walked toward the phone but still did not pick it up. You saw them swinging into what looked like the bedroom.

You wished you could be invisible. You wished your phone was a gun. You wished you had enough gas to pour round the house and set it ablaze. You wished you could invoke the tornado of 1952 on the house. You wetted your fingers with your saliva and rubbed your eyes. You were not dreaming. You called again. This time, the male figure did not walk toward the phone. He switched off the light as the two figures gently landed on what must be the bed. You knew exactly what would follow. You have been there.

You started your car and drove away as erratic as a sliced worm, wondering amongst other things if he had given her a tattoo too. And if so, what her tattoo might say; Scumbag?

As you drove home, tears trickled down your eyes. Every mile away from Worcester, its seven steep hills fading behind, you imagined the undertakers preparing your first love for burial. This is one funeral you will not attend. You had waited for eternity for those tears to flow. Now you feared it would flood Lake Quinsigamond. But weeping was all your soul needed to be free.

At Tobin Bridge, across the Mystic River of Massachusetts, the spirits of those who could not bear loads like this besieged you. They said, "Stop the car. Climb out. Take a jump off the bridge. Immerse your tired body into this cold water. It will cool your soul." There were many voices. They were loud, cluttered and making eerie noises across the cantilever truss. You heard a voice like that of Charles Stuart. His murdered pregnant wife sobbed in the background. You heard a splash as his body made the 115 ft. plunge into the river, causing receding ripples just as Boston police circled his home.

You slowed down your car. You pulled up by the emergency lane. You clicked the door open with your tear soaked hands. The night was chilly. You looked out and saw darkness as creepy as a monster's claws. Suddenly, the voices stopped shouting and began to whisper in seductive tones.
You put your foot out and it felt unsteady touching the frozen bridge.

From afar, you heard police sirens singing a dirge. They were coming toward you. They were driving up fast. You ducked into the car like a scared snail burying its head in the shell. You started the car and drove off in a panic. The voices jumped into the car with you and began to call you a coward. You assured them you were not a coward. You debated with them. They insulted you. You continued to drive, fidgeting and frightened. You turned on the radio to interrupt the voices. On the radio, the alternative rock band, Failure came on. They were singing 'The Nurse Who Loved Me':

> *Say hello to everything you've left behind*
> *It's even more a part of your life now that*
> *you can't touch it*
> *I'm taking her home with me, all dressed in white*
> *She's got everything I need; some pills in a little cup*
> *She's fallen hard for me; I can see it in her eyes...*

Those were the last words you heard before you smashed into a pavement a few yards off the bridge.

The Butcher, the Surgeon and I

On a sunny Thanksgiving afternoon, I stood in the kitchen of my Southern California home, heating a quart of oil in a saucepan and mixing onions, peppers and a castor seed condiment, *ogiri*, in a soup plate. It was the last *ogiri* in the house, one of the food items I looked forward to replenishing when I got the chance.

Warming inside the oven was a turkey delivered by caterers, and four pieces of plantain I had roasted earlier. I poured the hot vegetable oil into the mix, wishing I had the palm oil used by Nkanu women to make the tastiest plantains on the sidewalks of Enugu. Ideally, I would have added the vegetables into the saucepan, watched them sizzle and stirred the mix with a wooden spatula, but not in this house.

In order to reduce the smell emanating from the dish, an aroma that the initiated find pleasant but others find disgusting, I quickly covered the plate with a saucer. Some of the smell however escaped so I quickly grabbed a hand fan and began to direct it away from the window to the backyard where my wife was playing with our grandchildren. The fan was not doing a good job so I hurried upstairs to the bathroom to pick up a can of air freshener. When I returned to the kitchen, I found my soup plate in the sink.

"Even today!" I said to my wife as she leaned on the fridge, frowning. "On Thanksgiving day, on our 40th anniversary, you could not even indulge me, Georgina?"

My two sons Cal and Williams were standing at the bar, holding their noses. My daughter Brenda was busy opening the windows and spraying two cans of air freshener at the same time. My oldest grandchild, Cal Jr., looked at my face and asked in his eight-year-old voice, "Grandpa, were you planning to eat that thing? It smells like rotten cheese."

The boy had my broad nose, big ears and oval face. His hair was curled and dark like that of the Nkanu warriors of years past. His brown eyes skipped two generations to look like those of my father. In spite of the resemblance, I felt I was alone in this family – cut off from everyone.

"You all should leave grandpa alone," said Brenda's six-year old daughter, Brittney. "All grandpas do the things they like. That's what makes a grandpa a grandpa."

As she spoke, her blue eyes shone. With her long face and rosy cheeks, she looked a lot like Georgina in her kid picture.

"That's my girl," I said as she ran across the kitchen into my waiting arms.

I picked her up, kissed her forehead and rubbed her long hair. I swung her around while singing the chorus of the Temptations' song, "My Girl", as we made our way to the living room.

I overheard Williams say he thought the caterers brought some fabulous Thanksgiving meals.

"As he gets older, he gets worse," my wife said to the children. "If I let him have his way, he will start behaving like his butcher father and this house will be a refuse dump." "What do neighbours say when they see you in the morning?" Cal asked.

"Nice flavour you had going last night," my wife said.

"What was it you were cooking? Goat meat?"

"Do they really find the odour pleasant?" Williams asked.

"Of course not," my wife said. "They make fun of us."

"But Mummy," Brenda said, "you used to love those odd things about Dad."

"For a while, odd is exotic," my wife answered. "But if it

lingers, it becomes disgusting."

"But some of that will always be part of our heritage," Brenda said.

"The problem with idealism is that it pretends not to have any limit," my wife replied. "I've got to the limit of idealism and there is nowhere else to go."

I showed Brittney the people in the pictures lining the walls of the living room.

"This is your great grandfather," I said to her pointing at my father's black and white picture. "He was a great man when he was alive."

"What did he do?" Brittney asked.

"He taught me how to be a surgeon before I went to medical school," I answered.

I overheard the conversation in the kitchen.

"I am happy I did not buy into this whole African thing," Williams said.

"Not even with the Obama phenomenon?" Cal asked.

"I have never been tempted to," Williams said. "I find it hard to embrace backwardness." For a moment, Williams sounded like I did when I first came to America.

I heard someone turn on the sink's waste disposer.

"Who's this?" Brittney asked, pointing at my mother's picture.

"She is your great grandmother," I said.

"Was she great, too?" Brittney asked.

"She was a great home maker."

"What does that mean?"

"She made everyone around her feel at home."

"Oh."

The screeching of the disposer drowned the chattering in the kitchen. I carried Brittney over to the entertainment centre and turned on the stereo.

"Ready to dance with grandpa?" I asked.

"Yes."

I put her down as the music of the Temptations filled the

room. I held Brittney's hand. She twisted her body around as we began to dance.

At the end of 'My Girl', a few seconds before 'Just My Imagination' began to play, I saw Cal Jr. standing at the base of the staircase sucking his thumb.

I have practiced obstetrics and gynaecology in Los Angeles for over thirty-five years. I often performed surgery on pregnant women whose babies were days behind their due dates. Some of the babies I delivered have graduated from medical school. I have three homes. The first is in Nkanu, Nigeria, the second is in Cerritos, California and the third is in Enugu, Nigeria.

I take vacations twice a year. I usually spend the winter in sunny Africa and the summer in Europe, Asia or Latin America. I have done so every year for the last twenty-nine years. As I got older, historic sites in other parts of the world fascinated me less. I have seen them all. Their once lovely smells have now turned into the stench of their brutal histories. I am no longer an innocent tourist who sees the fresh paints and not the graffiti they cover. I see ghosts hanging on rooftops of palaces. On the skies above the edifices, I see blood hovering around the clouds like a dirty rainbow. At the foot of great pillars, I see footprints of slaves and ponds of sweat lost as they hauled the stones that built those monuments. It troubles me. It stopped me from seeing the fluttering wings of the pigeons. It stopped me from buying souvenirs for those who could not see the real thing. It stopped me from enjoying the delicacies served at restaurants near these historical sites.

I have not always been like this. I believed in Western civilization. It saved my life. I once vouched for it. I once thought the Enlightenment was the greatest gift the West gave to the world. I believed it was what differentiated the West from many other societies, including my hometown, Nkanu. In my quiet moments, I believed I would bring enlightenment to my own people. That was why for the last five years, I have been considering returning to my hometown permanently. I felt it would be a good place to retire. My decision has nothing to do with the transformation the practice of medicine is going through in America. It is irritating, but I am too old to care. I pay my malpractice insurance and as much as possible; I protect myself with a whole lot of paperwork and still manage to make a good living. My strategy is to do little direct patient-doctor work. I am a consultant at the University of California teaching hospitals. Young doctors surround me most of the time. But I am also tired.

Part of the reason why I am homeward bound has to do with my children and my wife. Georgina, my wife of forty years is now like one of those monuments of Europe. She is of high value to our visitors, but for me, she is just there. She no longer inspires me to dare. Our lives, our home and our acquaintances in Cerritos are all in her image.

Except for when I travel to Nkanu, she is in total control of my life.

Last Christmas, amongst our visitors was a colleague of mine, Dr. Ikedife, from Malibu, California. I went into the kitchen to make plantains with my famous sauce. I peeled eight plantains in quick succession. I rubbed light vegetable oil and salt on each one and placed them inside the oven for forty-five minutes during which time they became brown and soft inside. I brought out onions I had kept inside the refrigerator for twenty minutes. I peeled them without tearing up. I diced the onions into tiny cubes and also chopped red Mexican peppers. When the oil was about the right temperature, I poured in the mix. It sizzled, letting out a mixture of aromas. White smoke quickly engulfed the kitchen. Georgina was so disgusted with the pungency of the *ogiri* that she poured the sauce into the sink and splashed water on it. She did not care that Dr. Ikedife was watching.

"Never when we have company," she said after she saw how gloomy her action made Dr. Ikedife and I.

On this Thanksgiving Day, I did not invite Dr. Ikedife. I thought my children and grandchildren were family and did not count as company. Evidently, I was wrong.

I met Georgina at the State University of New York at Buffalo, New York. It was 1968 and interracial romance was uncommon.

"What's the meaning of Okons?" she asked, the first time we met in an English 101 class. I had to explain to her that Okons was not my real name. It was an abbreviated form of my full name, Okonkwo.

"Why did you abbreviate your name?" she asked.

"To make it easy for Americans to pronounce," I said.

"If Americans had a problem with your skin colour would you bleach your skin?" she asked.

That was how our relationship started. For a teenager from tropical Africa stuck in freezing Buffalo, she was my fireplace, keeping me warm with her smile, her energy and her love for life. No wonder we had two kids, Brenda and Cal, even before I graduated from Medical school. Her studies were interrupted by the kids' arrival. But she eventually graduated from the school of pharmacy. We moved to California in 1975 where we had our third child, Williams. She stopped practising pharmacy many years ago when she began helping manage my medical practice. These days she does voluntary work at the Museum of Science in Pasadena, California.

Georgina has aged. Contours of wrinkles line her face. Under her eyes are bags of tears that were never shed. I once offered to pay for a facelift. She did not speak to me for weeks. When she was younger, men skipped work just to soak in her beauty. She had blonde hair that once reached down to her shoulders. She stood on tall legs; like a flamingo. She was one surprise I never expected. At college, those resentful of our relationship called us Queen Elizabeth and Idi Amin.

I wasn't blessed with good looks. But I had a well-built frame that even my worst enemy acknowledged. My bones were strong, and connected a network of sturdy muscles developed from years of felling trees with axes, climbing up the hill with buckets of water fetched at the village stream, Ngene, and slaughtering goats.

Yes, before I became a surgeon, I was a village boy who knew how to sharpen and wield a knife. Before I opened books on anatomy and physiology, I had opened up the carcasses of hundreds of goats. This surgeon who delivered babies by caesarean operations had in the past gone into the bellies of goats with almost the same skills. Before I spent years in medical school, I had learned the importance of each body part on my father's butcher's table. The elders of Nkanu did not joke with their goat meat. The kidney was important to them the same way the placenta is to a pregnant woman. The gall bladder must be cut off with great care lest it burst and ruined the taste of surrounding parts of the meat with the bitterness of its bile. Every bone of a goat was accounted for. Even the intestines were cleaned out and shared. I had singlehandedly cut up many goats given to the village as marriage gifts in my last two years at home. I had spread out each body part delicately on banana leaves. The ribs were sliced up according to the number of families in our clan. The waist, carved out in the right manner, was reserved for the daughters of the village. Elders inspected the process like attending physicians, frowning at errors and barking at misplaced portions.

I was headed for Afor Ogbete market to begin a career as a butcher when I won a scholarship to study in America.

Be it Oye Olisa, Afor Igwe, Nkwo Nnewi, Oye Agu, Afor Nnobi, or Nkwo Agbaja, whatever market there was east of the Niger and beyond, my people dominated the butchery business. We monopolized it. When we went in, others went out. I had done my apprenticeship at Afia Ogbete where my father was a well-known butcher. After school, on weekends and on holidays, I would go to my father's stall to help him. I made my mark on goats amidst vultures and hordes of flies.

I used to get to my father's stall early in the evening, take off my school uniform in a kiosk behind the stall and put on my khaki shorts and jumper. I would tie my white apron, now stained to an unnameable colour with goats' blood round my waist; wash my hands and step up to the cutting table. My father would move out of the stall in order to give me room to take over. He often took time off to sniff some tobacco as lines of Nkanu women formed in front of his stall.

"How is our favourite school boy doing today?" the women would demand as I performed my preparatory rituals that included washing the knives, covering garbage bins, spraying disinfectants and air fresheners. Some love-struck women would say, "Show us those sturdy muscles of yours."

I used to smile. The arm muscles would pop up as soon as I grabbed the first lump of meat.

My father's competitors murmured that I attracted these women with voodoo. They called on the women to come to their stalls and get better deals, but the women would stay in line even as competitors screamed the price-busting slogan, "*Mgbuka! Mgbuka*! Buy one and get one free." My father would nudge me to reduce the portion of meat I cut for some of these women customers. I was about to take on cows when my scholarship letter arrived.

My only brother, Ezeagu, was bright at school, too. Just like me, he learnt the skills required to run our father's stall. He also learnt to study hard, sometimes burning the proverbial midnight candle quite literally with his feet in a pail of water. When I left Nigeria before the Nigeria-Biafra civil war began in 1966, he was still in secondary school. He fought in the war as a child soldier, working with the intelligence group called the Boys' Company. These were children who crossed the enemy lines and sent information back to the Biafran side. He got shot in his right leg after a captured Biafran soldier under torture blew the cover of the Boys' Company. The bullet lodged in his bone causing him to limp. He could not go back to school after the war. He lost the desire to study. I tried to encourage him with materials and funds but he suffered severely from posttraumatic stress disorder. He returned to our father's stall at Ogbaete market and continued the legacy.

For years, he was the head of the butchers association of Ogbaete. Now he manages our family compound. Though I ensure he is well taken care of, he still insists on living the village life. He loved to climb palm trees to tap for the sweet frothy white wine.

The pogrom that led to the civil war made me believe that black people were heartless butchers who deserved no place in civilized societies. I lost two uncles in Northern Nigeria's pogrom against the Igbo. They were butchered by knife wielding Hausa men. My Nkanu people worked with knives too. But they didn't go about cutting down innocent people to settle political quarrels. I lost both my parents during the civil war that followed. My father died of kwashiorkor, a disease that normally kills malnourished children. His death brought shame to all of us because he had a protruding stomach before he died. Before the British occupation, people with an affliction like his were dumped in the evil forest and left to die. My mother was raped by occupying Nigerian soldiers who overran our hometown at the early stages of the war. She later died of heartbreak. I did not want anything to do with black people until Georgina convinced me otherwise. At first, I thought she was one of those who allowed white guilt over slavery to overshadow their reasoning. But she persistently made her point ever so gently that I began to reconsider.

"Do you understand what happened at the Berlin conference," she asked in those early days. "Yes. The Scramble for Africa," I answered.

"Do you really understand it?"

"Yes, I do." I said quickly, trying to avoid a lecture.

"It is like having a meeting in Mecca and the Emir of Kuwait declaring that the whole of North America, Canada, the United States and Mexico were his personal property. That was what

King Leopold of Belgium did."

"And so?" The question had come out of my mouth before I realized that I had invited a lecture.

"He basically claimed a land that was over eighty times larger than his kingdom and brought several diverse peoples with different cultures and languages together as one country," she said. "No input from the people. Just like that."

"But African people should be over that by now," I said.

"Yes, they tried. Patrice Lumumba tried. But what happened? The same Europeans murdered him and in his place they installed their puppet, Mobutu."

"You are correct."

"It was not always the making of black people," she said.

"There were always powerful external instigators and willing local thugs in whose hands black people were often helpless."

When I first went back home in 1979, Georgina was the one who insisted on the trip. She liked it then. It was a relatively prosperous Nigeria, quiet and promising. We returned each year, the last being in 1984, a year after the military took over power again.

We had a peaceful Christmas holiday at Nkanu. Our kids enjoyed life in the village setting as well as the days we spent in the city. We arrived at Eko Meridian Hotel in Ikoyi, Lagos, for the last leg of our journey on Boxing Day.

On the last Saturday of the year, Georgina and I got a call from Dr. Ikedife, who was spending his holidays at the Lekki beach area of Lagos Island. He had asked us to visit him at his newly completed house. We climbed into our rented car, pulled out of Adetokunbo Ademola Street and set out on our way.

The roads were free of vehicular traffic. The notorious Lagos Island traffic was not to be seen. The drive along the Island was as smooth as a drive on the Los Angeles freeways on

Super Bowl day. The ghettos of Maroko and Ajegunle with their shanty houses were off the radar. Lagos Island had modern bungalows, expensive mansions and an extensive well-graded road network. Populated by top government functionaries and rich businessmen, including foreign nationals, the lawns were manicured the way they were done in the wealthy parts of the western capitals.

"Maybe we should build a house here and retire to its quiet neighborhood," Georgina said.

The gentle breeze from the beach was cruising in and out of our car through the open windows.

"You mean it?" I asked.

"Yes," Georgina said. "It is beautiful here and very quiet."

"I told you that the military boys are cleaning up the country."

"You won't say so if you were among the young students they executed at that beach recently."

"They were drug traffickers," I said.

"They don't deserve death."

"Africans need a strong hand that will mould them into a civilized people."

"Listen to what you're saying."

"I'm serious. Some people must pay a price for the transformation of a society" I insisted.

"Will you pay a price if asked to?"

I thought about Georgina's question as we passed through Eleke Crescent where many foreign embassies were located. If anyone was blindfolded and dropped there, they would never imagine this was somewhere in Africa. The architecture in these parts looked foreign; the flowers on the perimeters were tropical but were groomed with a touch of western expertise. The Crescent stood in the shadows of the Marina where modest skyscrapers provided proof that the multinationals have long arrived.

We headed to Lekki Road along the Lekki-Epe Expressway. We were halfway across the Mobil petrol station when a roadblock confronted us. There were two cars in front of us and the occupants were sitting on the ground by the roadside. They had their hands on their heads. Standing beside them were half a dozen heavily armed soldiers. They flagged us down, signalling us to stop. I stepped on the brakes.

"Step out of the car, Mister," screamed one of the soldiers.

"What's wrong?" I asked.

"I said step out of the car."

"Anything wrong?" I asked again.

"Are you deaf?" the soldier asked looking agitated.

I stepped out.

"You mistress too," the soldier demanded.

"That's my wife," I said.

"*Na you sabi*," the soldier dismissed in his heavily accented Pidgin English.

"What's going on?" Georgina asked.

"Honey, please step out of the car," I said.

She stepped out.

"What's wrong officer?" I asked.

"Go sit down there," the soldier yelled.

He walked away.

I stood there with Georgina looking at a young couple on the floor with their hands on their heads. At the other end of the road was an elderly man with his driver sitting on the asphalt sidewalk.

"What's going on?" Georgina asked me.

"I don't know. But I will soon find out," I said. The soldier soon returned after conferring with his superior sitting in a kiosk beside the roadblock.

"So you two are too good to sit down?" he asked.

"There is no seat here," Georgina said.

"I get it," the soldier said. "Your white butt is too pretty to sit on an African ground?"

"Let us sit down," I said to Georgina.

"I am not sitting on the ground," she said firmly.

I stooped a little. The soldier stormed toward us. I dropped my knees and found myself kneeling on the ground. I tried to pull Georgina down but she pulled her hands away.

The soldier got to us in three steps.

"Lady, sit down!" he yelled.

"I'm not sitting on the ground," Georgina replied, unfazed. In one swoop, the soldier kicked both her feet, flinging her to the ground. Georgina landed on her backside. She let out a cry and then a series of sobs.

"Put your hands on your head," the solider ordered.

"Bloody idiots!"

We obeyed.

"What is wrong, officer?" I asked. "What did we do wrong?"

"You broke the law," the soldier said.

"What law?" I asked.

"Don't you know we are in a war?" the soldier asked.

"What war?" I asked.

"The war against indiscipline," he answered.

"So what law did we break?" I asked.

"Law against indiscipline," he answered.

"What does the law say?" I asked.

"That you should not drive on Environmental Sanitation Day," the soldier said. "You should be home cleaning your house."

"But we are staying in a hotel," I said.

"And so?" the soldier muttered as he walked back to the kiosk.

I had heard about the sanitation day but had never experienced it. It was part of a series of edicts the military had put in place to bring order and structure to society. I was an initial supporter of the reforms because I saw how people were lining up at bus stops and at the post office and I liked it. It looked more and more like a civilized society. I had dismissed criticism from the elite that the military were abusing civilians in the course of instituting these transformations.

The soldier returned. He asked us to form a straight line. And we did. He ordered us to walk up and down the expressway picking up litter. When we were done, he asked us to open the trunk of our cars and dump the thrash in there. Georgina walked beside me. She cursed all the way. She was loud at first until the soldier confronted her.

"If you curse one more time, I will throw you into the bush," he warned.

Then, he burst into a tirade.

"This is not the World Bank. This is not the United Nations. This is not one of those fucking institutions where your country humiliates developing countries like ours. This is Lagos. Your cowboy president can wake up and bomb sleeping children of Libya but he cannot do shit here. This is Lagos. We said we do not want to owe you guys anymore. We want to pay you off. And you said no, we must owe you. What kind of nonsense is this? We want to be free of your debt. We want to determine our fate but hell no. You want to keep us tied down. So much for 'all men are created equal.'"

When he was done, Georgina's curses had watered down into whispers.

I noticed that some cars were allowed to pass the roadblock without the occupants being asked to step out. Most of these where military vehicles, painted dark green, with military brass sitting in the well-upholstered backseats. Others were civilian vehicles with federal government number plates. I saw few private vehicles too with what seemed like very important personalities in the back seats cruise through the roadblock without so much as a second look from the soldiers. A thought came to me when one of the occupants of a newly stopped vehicle was taken to the kiosk to make a call. Thereafter, he was allowed to drive off.

"Officer," I called out.

He turned around and looked at me. He did not say a word.

"Could I make a phone call, please?" I asked.

"To whom?"

"Brigadier Ikedife is waiting for us at his home," I said.

"I want to let him know we are delayed." The soldier blinked repeatedly.

"Brigadier who?" he asked.

"Brigadier Ikedife," I repeated.

He hurried up to the kiosk and conferred with his superior.

"Who's Brigadier Ikedife?" Georgina whispered.

"Dr. Ikedife's brother," I answered.

"Do you know him?"

"No."

"Do you have his number?"

"No."

"What will you do if they allow you to call him?"

"I will call Dr. Ikedife."

It was a gamble I needed to take because the soldiers were not relenting and Georgina's skin was beginning to turn red as the sun emerged. We held our breaths as we watched the soldier confer with his superior. Minutes later, he returned.

"*Oga, make una dey go,*" he said in Pidgin English.

Georgina refused to follow me home ever since. As her faith in Nigeria and anyone's ability to rescue it faded, mine increased. She never returned home with me even after I had built a mansion in the exclusive Government Reserved Area of Enugu. It was an edifice, a manifestation of wealth that would have made my father yell my grandfather's title name, "*Aku rue uno.*" Nothing I did could convince Georgina to give Nigeria another try.

"I've turned you into an African extremist," Georgina said the last time I raised the topic.

"What do you mean by that?" I asked.

"My prayers were answered," she said, "but by then I had started a new prayer."

I had wanted to repeat the cliché about being careful what you prayed for… but I held off because Georgina hated clichés. Her greatest strength was in knocking down truism.

"You bought what I was selling," she said to herself.

"Georgina, please look at it this way," I pleaded. "I still have life in me and can still do some good. But if I stay here, I'm heading straight for the nursing home."

"You can still do some good here."

"But nobody really wants me here or even needs me. I'm replaceable. There are thousands of people like me here. But there, my little contributions will have a multiplier effect."

"What about your family?" she asked.

"Why will you choose to abandon them? Is it for fear of the nursing home or this unknown need over there?"

By the 90s, our kids had grown up and left home. Brenda is a doctor practicing in Alaska where she lives with her husband, also a doctor. Cal is a pilot with Air France. He is married to a French air hostess and they live at Long Island, New York and also in Paris. Our last child Williams is a struggling actor in Hollywood. They all stopped going to Nigeria with me when their mother stopped. Not even Williams, who lives nearby, showed up at our house in Cerritos during the holidays. They have all moved on with their lives and once or twice a month I get a phone call from Brenda who would often share brief anecdotes of my grandchildren with me. If anybody had been abandoned, it was I. And as my father used to say, he who others have rejected must not reject himself.

In 1999, I began a free medical mission to Nigeria. I got together doctors, nurses and medical supplies and for two weeks we travelled across Eastern Nigeria providing free medical services to the rural folk. During each visit, I look out for what I could possibly do if I returned to Nigeria permanently. I still dream about bringing that enlightenment Georgina used to talk about. It was in that spirit that I gave my support to a contestant for the kingship title in my hometown. This was the first contest since the rule was changed to stop making the succession hereditary; as was set up by the British colonial power. I supported the candidate who promised to eradicate the Osu caste system that tagged some citizens free born and others slaves. The slaves were denied full rights of citizenship. It was a controversial and emotional issue that made the traditionalists angry when my candidate was named the king-elect.

Georgina knows about my medical mission to Nigeria. I thought it would touch the humanitarian spirit in her. But she does not care. Our home in Cerritos is a beautiful one-storey building. We have a visiting housekeeper, a gardener and can afford any service we need. Our dog, Mannie, is as old as Georgina. The once energetic American pointer hardly barks anymore. It does not even wag its tail when I come home.

Mannie barked three times on Thanksgiving Eve; each time for when the doorbell rang and each of our kids arrived with a bouquet of flowers. We saw our grandchildren for the first time in three years. Brenda had two, Brittney and Stephen, and Cal had one, Cal Jr. Williams, I suspected was gay. He came with his 'friend.'

Cal's wife had not changed much from the way she looked on her wedding day some eight years ago. She still had her smile and walked with the same elegance. If I had never seen old air hostesses, I would have declared that air hostesses never aged. Maybe they age slower than other people. I get along well with my daughter-in-law. She radiates courtesy and still has her sense of humour.

"Is the air in the first class cabin really different from the air in the coach," I once asked her.

"No, Dr. Okons," she said. "The air in all the cabins is the same. The only place where the air is different is in the cockpit."

"Why is that?" I asked.

"Because pilots fart," she said.

"Everyone farts," I said.

"Sometimes," she said. "But pilots fart all the time." If her pilot husband was not within hearing distance I would have discounted that.

Brenda's husband was a lot like me. As a doctor, he had an unobstructed look at the ins and outs of life. He must have adjusted to accommodate my daughter, who is not different from her mother.

He once cornered me at the balcony upstairs and asked. "Dr. Okons, what is the secret to a long happy married life?" This was before the incident in the kitchen.

"It is simple," I said. "Do no harm, keep the pain secret and keep away from every seduction."

"Is the answer in the oath?"

"Well, it is like the oath," I said.

"The Hippocratic oath?" he asked.

"No. The other one."

"Which one?"

"The one they call a vow," I said. "You know the difference between an oath and a vow?"

"No," Brenda's husband replied.

"If you violate an oath, you lose your license."

"Aha."

"But if you violate a vow, you lose half your estate."

It was our first heart-warming get-together in years. Our home was lively. Kids were running around, making noise and breaking things. Dinner was served just after the first football game ended and the second was about to start. The Cowboys and the Seahawks again divided the family. Everyone, but Brittney and I were on the side of the Cowboys.

Assorted dishes covered our formal dinning table. Occupying the center was the turkey. It stood out like a fountain surrounded by flowers. There was stuffing, glazed ham, mashed potatoes, peas, carrots and green beans. There was also cranberry compote, gravy, rolls, creamed corn, sausages, strawberry truffle and chocolate cake. Even though every inch of space on the table was taken up, I missed my plantain and sauce.

"This family has come a long way," I prayed. "With tentacles all over the world, may we give back some of the great things in life that we have received through our Lord Jesus."

The Amens I heard were very few. There was definitely nothing heard from the spot where Williams and his friends were sitting.

"Why can't we do this once a year?" I asked, afterwards.

"We cannot fly down here every year," Cal said.

"Why?" I asked. "Have they stopped paying pilots well?"

"It's not about money," Cal said.

"So what is it about? Fear of flying?" I asked.

Brittney smiled.

"Forget it," said Cal.

"We can rotate it," I said. "We can visit any of you in turns." I looked at my wife and saw her roll her eyes.

"Where will that leave your endless trips to Africa in pursuit of who-knows-what?" she asked, the sarcasm evident in her voice.

"I want to go to Africa too," Brittney said. "I want to visit Madagascar and the Lion King countries."

Sitting all around the dining table in our formal wear with chandeliers lit up above, ours was a picturesque family. Looking back to where I came from, I could see I had indeed come a long way. But looking forward to where my family was headed, I feared it wasn't my destination. Maybe it was the way it should be. But nothing had prepared me for this; getting where I had always wanted to be only to yearn for where I started.

"I will host the next get together," Cal said. "We can meet anytime in our house in Long Island."

"Why not Paris?" Brenda asked.

"If you all are up to that, so am I, hey" Cal said.

"My passport has expired," Williams chipped in.

"Then renew it," Brenda riposted.

"We will work out the details after dinner," I said.

As prearranged, my children's spouses and their kids went out to see a movie after dinner. I had wanted to be with wife and children alone as we discussed my future plans. I was seriously considering spending more time in Nigeria in pursuit of my philanthropic goals. There was also talk about getting a political appointment in the health ministry.

"In the course of human events, there comes a time when a man must answer to his father's name," I began as soon as the front door closed.

"This is going to be interesting," said my wife. "It has transformed from there comes a time when a man must use his tongue to count his teeth to there comes a time when…"

"As opposed to using his teeth to count his tongue?" Brenda interjected.

Carl and Williams all laughed.

The eyes of my children looked like those of kids waiting to hear their father's will. I ignored the snide remarks because all I had said was that I was at a juncture in life when I needed to take stock of my life. I continued.

"You have all grown to be secure and responsible adults," I said, scanning their faces. I made sure my eyes focus more on Cal and Brenda.

"No proverbs, please," my wife said.

"But Mummy, you used to love them when we were small," Brenda said.

"Used to…" Georgina pointed out.

"I will be going to Nigeria on Sunday. I'm exploring career opportunities over there" I continued.

"Why?" Cal asked.

"He is afraid of staying here and ending up in a nursing home," my wife said, her disdain once again seeping through. "Where do old people end up over there in Nigeria?" Williams asked. He was looking at his mother for an answer.

"I don't know," my wife said.

"Like I was saying, I think I have something left in me to give and I think giving to those who have little to nothing is the best gift there is," I said.

"While you're at it, tell the kids about your name change," my wife said.

"Dad, you changed your name?" Cal asked.

"Yes," I said.

"To what?" Williams asked.

"To Okonkwo," I said.

"Oko what?" Williams quizzed.

"What's wrong with Okons?" Brenda asked.

"I don't know what it means," I said.

"Wait a minute," Cal said. "But that is your name and our name."

"Yes," I said. "It was a mockery of my real name."

"Which is what?" Williams asked.

"Okonkwo," I said.

"Does that mean I have to change my name?" Williams asked.

"You don't have to unless you want to" I assured them.

A long silence descended on the meeting. It was the type of silence that seemed to say this was a much more serious issue than we had thought.

In the middle of the preface to my talk I got a call. It was from my nephew in Nigeria.

"Excuse me," I said to my family. "This is from Nigeria." They shrugged.

"Uncle," my nephew said. "There is trouble."

"What happened?" I asked.

"The abominable," he said.

"What is it?"

"Ezeagu is dead."

"What?"

"He was murdered."

"By who?"

"By the opponents of the king-elect. They said they were getting back at you for funding his election."

"When did that happen?"

"Yesterday."

"Where?"

"He was tapping a palm tree for wine when they came for him," my nephew said in-between sobs. "They surrounded the palm tree and waited for him to climb down. He tapped his palm wine and descended from the tree carrying in his hands a gourd of fresh palm wine and his climbing rope. He shared his wine with the men who had gathered around him, each drinking from the gourd itself. Then they seized him. Their leader brought out the knife tied to his waist and cut off his head. They laid out banana leaves under the same palm tree cut up his body into small pieces as if they were cutting up the flesh of a goat."

I dropped the phone and told my family that my brother had been murdered by those determined to stop me from ever going home.

"Which brother?" they asked.

I had only one brother.

As I went upstairs, my mind was flooded by images of blood, body parts, babies, screams, and bones. Nobody followed me as I climbed the stairs. I laid down on my bed and cried for hours.

When I finally got up the next day, I walked out of my house without saying a word to my family. Brittney caught up with me at the door and wanted to follow me out.

"Come back here," Brenda yelled at her.

"I am going to Madagascar with grandpa," Brittney said.

"Get your behind here, right now!" Brenda yelled.

The family watched me climb down the stairs with a traveling bag in tow. None of them tried to stop me. I got into my car and drove off. I drove eighteen miles to the Los Angeles Airport clutching my KLM ticket to Lagos before it occurred to me that I was two days ahead of my scheduled travel date.

As I made my way back to the parking lot, I saw Dr. Ikedife loading his luggage into his wife's car.

"Coming back from home?" I asked.

"Yes," he answered. "Like I told you, it was a quick visit. I said goodbye to my old man who is dying of prostate cancer."

"Sorry to hear that," I said.

"Oh, he is old now," Dr. Ikedife said. "And something will always bring it to an end. If it is not cancer it will be something else."

For a moment, I missed my father. Maybe if he had lived longer, my life would have been different. Maybe I would have had more reason to get involved with activities at home earlier than now. Maybe Georgina would have persevered and given Nigeria another chance. Maybe my children would have had a reason to care about where I came from. I stopped myself from thinking how he would have viewed my present relationship with my family. In his world, a man was not supposed to be seen in the kitchen let alone be caught cooking. It would have been considered an abomination. In his world, a woman who refused to cook what a man wanted would dare not throw away a man's cooking. It would have been called a double abomination. My father would have considered my situation one in which dying would have been a better option.

"I can see you have your traveling bag, where to?" Dr. Ikedife asked me.

"I was scheduled to travel home in two days' time but I came to the airport today."

"Everything alright?" Dr. Ikedife asked.

"My brother was hacked to death yesterday," I said.

"Oh my God!" he exclaimed.

"Don't say that!" Ikedife's wife said.

"Yes. Some political thugs murdered him," I said.

"Is it safe for you to go home then?" Dr. Ikedife asked.

"I don't know," I replied.

"You have to think about your safety before you rush home," he advised.

"The possibility of dying does not stop people from going to war," I quipped.

"But good warriors choose their battles carefully," Dr. Ikedife said.

"If I don't go now, I may never go home again," I said.

"You should go home and bury your brother."

"Yes, I will."

"But it needs to be planned."

"Yes."

"Did your wife know what happened?" Dr. Ikedife asked.

"I told her."

"And she allowed you to head home?"

"She does not care."

"I'm sorry to hear this."

"Such is life."

"I think you should come with us," Dr. Ikedife said. "Let us go to my house for a while."

"Ok," I accepted almost without thinking.

"When we get home, I will call my brother. I will ask him to provide you with military escort from the airport to anywhere you go in Nigeria," Dr. Ikedife said.

"Until when?" I asked.

"Until you enter the plane for your journey back to the United States," he assured.

I had wanted to tell him that I had planned on going for good, but I held myself in check. If he would not move back home with his brother in the military, he would consider me crazy for thinking that, I guessed. I felt crazy just thinking about it. How could I live with those savages? What kind of security guarantee would make me do it?

Dr Ikedife climbed into his wife's car. I opened the back door, tossed my bag on the seat and climbed in too, as airport security staff waved the car on.

"Something smells like *ogiri* in this car," I said.

"I brought the original *ogiriokpi*," Dr. Ikedife said.

"Good," I said.

I closed my eyes and took in the aroma. My wandering brain stopped as soon as I made the concession. Home is not where you get back to. Home is where you are stuck.

The Attack of the Dwarfs

Emily was elated when the Southwest Airlines plane landed at Los Angeles. Getting away from New York was her only way of regaining sanity after three straight years of seventy-five hours a week nursing job. With her two-year-old son Okwy, and her mother it had been a torturous six-hour flight. Initially, the boy was excited, but he soon became restless as the flight progressed. The Boeing 737 proved to be too small a playground for him that everyone on the plane was relieved to see him fall asleep twenty minutes before touchdown.

With sleepy Okwy in her arms, her mother pushing the luggage cart, Emily scanned through the arrival lounge for her sister, Tessy. She had joked that Tessy might need a picture to recognize her. They hadn't seen each other since Emily's wedding, four years earlier. "One kid and three years of slaving as a nurse, it wears down one's body," Emily often said, "And no matter the best maintenance money can buy, the lines finally begin to show all over the place."

Tessy knew that Emily was exaggerating. She had seen Emily's email photographs and those in Africa Abroad newspapers, in which she was dancing away weekends alongside her stupendously dressed husband, Obiogaranya. Emily's defence had always been that it was their mother's arrival that allowed her time to go out and it was only on those few weekends when she was not working. But going by several newspaper pictures, Tessy knew it must have been lots of weekends.

Emily was searching for Tessy's number on her cell phone when she heard a familiar voice amongst those in the arrival lounge. She looked up and there was her sister with her five-year-old son in tow, hurrying up to them.

"Ada'm, my daughter, is this you?" their mother exclaimed. "This your country is huge. We fly all this way and still we are in one country." They all hugged and hugged again.

Tessy took Okwy from Emily and held him up, "He looks like ndi-Obosi," she said teasingly, referring to Obiogaranya's hometown, Obosi.

"Okwy, that's your aunty Tessy that you often speak to on the phone," Emily intervened, as Okwy struggled to free himself from Tessy. At the same time, Mama reached out to Tessy's son, Obumneme. She stretched her hands for a hug but Obumneme recoiled, holding tight to his mother's leg. Mama rubbed his head gently.

"My father," Mama said to Obumneme in reference to her own father who she believed reincarnated in Obumneme, "kedu ka imere?"

Obumneme looked away. Emily bent down to Obumneme's height and rubbed his cheek. "What's up little man?"

Again, Obumneme ignored her.

"Won't you say hello to Aunty Emily?" Emily tried again.

Obumneme kept her eyes focused on the ground; stealing a glance at Okwy now and then. Tessy noticed the awkwardness of the situation and came to the rescue. She handed Okwy back to Emily and picked Obumneme up. She introduced Obumneme to Emily, Okwy and her mother. It was then that Obumneme waved, in a way that seemed to Mama as weird.

Driving home through the stretches of highways and lights, like a passage in a star – littered sky, Emily, Tessy and Mama, reminisced, talking as if they had never spent hours on the phone.

"How is Obiogaranya?" Tessy asked.

"The man is full of...," Emily caught herself as she glanced at

Okwy, "He thinks he has brought a slave to America. It will all come to an end next year. And if that will be the end of the marriage, let it be. I am not working myself to death."

Mama raised her eyebrows and gave Emily a disapproving look. It was not the first time she was hearing this complaint but her position had always been that Emily should give the middle aged Obiogaranya more time to regain his footing in American society after losing his job. She believed that threatening and humiliating him was only aggravating the situation.

"I hear you, my sister," retorted Tessy.

"Don't encourage a bad thing, Theresa" Mama said.

"Mama, this is a modern world, different from your own time," responded Tessy, "that man should not be allowed to hit my sister again, ever."

"Not with her bad mouth. Sometimes, I do feel like hitting her myself," Mama said.

They drove for a while without saying anything. Okwy had fallen asleep again, and Obumneme sat quietly at the back of the Mercedes SUV, playing his Nintendo game.

"How doctor dey?" Emily asked, breaking the thick silence and changing the subject at the same time. Tessy's husband is an emergency room doctor.

"He dey. He is at work now. On Fridays, he comes home very late. But he is off this weekend so we will have time to explore LA."

"Is he still toying with the idea of going back home to run for political office?" Emily wondered.

"I don't know for him. I have told him in clear terms that he will be going alone. If he wants to go and be killed, let him go. I am staying put." Tessy responded, as a tinge of worry flashed across her face.

"Umu nwoke, men, things that pursue them are endless. If not this, it is that. Why would doctor want to go and mess with those people at home, ndi isi mebiri, the brain damaged. Why?" Mama questioned.

"Hasn't he heard about all these murders?" Emily chimed in. "Does he have a vaccine for that?"

"He says it is his calling," Tessy replied with resignation. "He thinks things are bad because good people like him chose to stay away and that if sacrifices have to be made to rescue his people, he should be one of those to make the sacrifice."

"Isi emebiera ya, has he become brain damaged, too?" Mama asked. "Does he want my daughter to be a widow? I will scream at him. If he is under any spell, we shall invoke the Holy Ghost fire to wipe it out. Tufiakwa! Damn it."

"Mama, don't get there and create any scene," Emily warned. "If he insists on running for elected office, let him go. Like many before him, the politicians at home will just take his money and spend. After the election, he will just come back here and begin again."

"That's where I stand now," Tessy interjected, "Let him try. He will be frustrated and he will be back here."

At Bayer Boulevard, Tessy pulled over in front of Panda Animal Clinic. She jumped out of the Mercedes SUV.

"Let me pick up our dog. It went for a physical check-up. I won't be long," Tessy said.

"Obumneme, stay with aunty and grandma. I will be right back."

"So your sister has a dog, too?" Mama asked. "A dog that goes to the hospital to see a doctor? Okwu agwugo, it's the end of story. So my daughter and her husband have joined these crazy Americans to care for dogs more than they care for other human beings? Eh? Is that why they have refused to have more children? They adopt homeless dogs but not homeless people. They spend more on pets than they spend on the needy. Odi egwu."

"Mama, they need a dog to help Obumneme learn socialization," Emily explained. "Some autistic children respond well when they learn to nurture pets."

Mama turned around from her chair and looked at Obumneme. She looked at him as if she was seeing him for the first time. Obumneme did not look up. He continued to fiddle with his Nintendo game.

"Did you say that medicine men at home would not help this boy?" Mama asked Emily in Igbo.

"I thought I have told you before that what he has is a medical condition, Mama. It is not something those crooked medicine men can cure."

"You all and your ogwu oyibo, western medicine. I just know that we don't have these at home, a boy who doesn't want to communicate with others."

"We do, mama. But not as rampant as they are here."

"Why is that? Why is it that every African family with four kids now has one of them? Are you sure these white people do not inject something into these kids?"

"And why would they do that?"

"Because they may be afraid that the way you have kids, you may soon overpopulate their country and take over everything. You know they only have one kid, one dog and one cat."

"If at all there is any group taking over, it is these Latinos you see everywhere," Emily said pointing at people moving around. "They are coming into the United States in their millions without visas and they are having kids like rabbits."

"Then they should be told to go after them and not the Africans who they hardly give any visas to come here."

"Mama, it is a disease that affects everyone, including white people."

"Then it must be something in the water."

"Something like what?"

"I don't know. All these things they concoct and make you eat and drink. I have always known that they came with side effects."

"They are seriously looking for the cure."

"I hope they find it fast. I can't stand to see my grandchild looking like this," Mama said, turning back again to look at Obumneme. He had not blinked from playing his game. "Chineke nalu ekwensu ike, may God take away power from the devil!"

Tessy walked out of the clinic carrying a mini poodle. The poodle looked like something seen in glossy magazines warming the arms of Hollywood actresses.

"Oh, that's so cute," said Emily.

Mama frowned.

"You can say it Mama," chided Emily. "Try a compliment sometimes – like, this is not nkita eke uke, poorly bred Uke dog."

Emily took the dog from Tessy and held it in her arms.

"Remind me of her name?"

"Lola," said Tessy.

Mama watched in horror as Lola licked Tessy's hands and face, her fur shining like some Christmas light.

"Uchu gba a," muttered Mama, as Tessy pulled into the driveway of her house. It was a gigantic colonial house on a two-acre land. The lawns were immaculate like pictures seen on postcards. On the front was a garden of roses and lilies. On both sides of the house were other gigantic houses, the type one sees at FESTAC extension in Lagos or the exclusive parts of Abuja.

Tessy stepped down from the SUV and opened the back door. She helped Obumneme come down. Obumneme held tight to his Nintendo. Lola jumped around him, wagging her tail. Emily went to the back of the car and unbuckled Okwy from the car seat. He was still sleeping.

"Let me open the door for you, Emily, so that you can go upstairs and put Okwy down," counselled Tessy. "I will come back to get your luggage."

"He should wake up now. He has slept enough, or he won't let someone sleep at night," said Emily.

"Oh o oh, how many of you live in this huge house?" asked Mama, bewildered.

"It's not that big. Wait till you see some of our neighbours' houses," responded Tessy.

Emily nudged Okwy to wake, but he wouldn't. Tessy opened the front door and Emily went in and laid Okwy down on the couch. She went back out and helped Tessy to bring in their luggage.

"How many rooms are in this house?" Mama asked, as she walked in behind Obumneme and Lola, looking mesmerized at the cathedral roof and ceiling made of glass.

"Just five," Tessy replied.

"And the rest are what?" Mama asked, still baffled.

"Library, game room, study, exercise room, laundry room, kitchen, dining, second living room, and ordinary rooms like that," Tessy answered. "I will show you around as soon as we get the luggage in."

Tessy and Emily brought the luggage in and took them up to the visitor's room. Emily had packed three boxes as if she was going on a one-year vacation.

Downstairs, Mama walked around the living room area looking at pictures and paintings that lined the wall; doctor at his graduation, doctor speaking to a group of white people, the wedding of doctor and Tessy at All Saints Cathedral in Onitsha, Tessy's father, Ugonnaya, Mama and Obumneme when he was just a toddler. She passed beside a large plasma TV that seemed plastered to the wall. She touched it gently, as if to affirm it was real.

She walked past, a fountain at one end of the living room and gently let the water splash on her fingers.

Obumneme sat at one end of the living room sofa playing his game. Lola hopped around him. Suddenly Obumneme flipped his game box on the wood floor. It made a huge noise that woke Okwy up.

Okwy opened his eyes and looked confused. Lola barked continuously from the landing of the staircase. Mama held Okwy tight. "Nwa m, iteta go, have you woken, my baby," she said.

Okwy nodded. He appeared tense and confused.

"We are at your aunt Tessy's place," Mama assured him.

Lola continued to bark, this time away from the step, toward the area where Mama and Okwy sat. Lola looked terrified.

"Teresa," Mama called out, "Come and control this dog. It barks as if it is seeing some spirits."

Okwy's body began to tremble with fear. He quivered like a baby about to convulse. Mama carried him up and held him to her chest.

"Ozugo, it's okay. It is only a dog." Mama said.

Tessy rushed down stairs. She found Obumneme seated quietly at a corner, looking down the floor as if he was watching an interesting film on the floor.

"Lola," Tessy called out, "Lola, will you come here and sit down. And keep quiet."

Lola ignored Tessy and kept barking. Tessy walked swiftly toward Lola and picked her up. In her hands, she continued to bark.

Suddenly, Okwy began to scream. As he screamed he kept pointing at the same end of the living room where Lola's eyes focused.

"Emily," Mama called out. "Emily come o! I don't know what is happening to Okwy."

Emily rushed down. Mama held Okwy's hands. Okwy continued to scream and Lola continued to bark. As Emily carried him upstairs, he kept on looking down, pointing and screaming.

"What is that?" asked Emily. "What?"

Okwy did not respond. He continued to cry uncontrollably.

"Do you want something to eat? Something to drink?"

Lola continued to bark.

"I will take Lola to the garage," Tessy said, carrying Lola with her. She opened the door that led to the garage and dropped Lola on the floor. Lola continued to bark as she slammed the door.

Emily carried Okwy downstairs again. She brought some of Obumneme's toys and waved them in Okwy's face. It did not stop him from screaming. She went to the fridge and brought him orange juice. It did not work. Mama took Okwy from her and carried him out of the house. In the driveway, Okwy finally stopped crying.

"I want my Daddy," he said to Mama.

"Your Daddy is in New York," Mama responded, "We are visiting aunty Tessy. Afterwards, we will go back and see Daddy."

"No, my Daddy, my Daddy," cried Okwy.

After a while, Okwy was calm. Emily came outside and carried him. She gave him orange juice. He drank. She gave him his favourite toy, Elmo, and he held it in his hands. But as soon as she opened the door for them to go back in, he began to cry and scream.

Emily took him inside despite his screams. "When he is tired he will stop crying," she said out of frustration.

In the living room, Okwy continued to cry and point at the floor. His temperature was rising.

Mama took him outside and once again, he stopped crying. Tessy opened the truck and let them sit inside.

Tessy and Emily consulted each other on what to do. They called doctor to see if he could come home but he was in with a patient. They decided to wait for doctor to call back before they made a decision.

"For two days now," Tessy confessed, "the dog has been barking like this. But when she is outside, she stops barking. That was why I took her to the vet to see if she has an infection or something."

"What could cause this?"

"I do not know."

Confused, Emily went to Obumneme and sat beside him. She watched him as he drew on an programmable notebook. She watched him draw tiny objects surrounding even smaller objects in the middle. He kept drawing different versions of the same thing. And each time, he erased them afterwards.

"Did you see what Obumneme has been drawing?" Emily asked Tessy.

"He has been drawing the same thing for the last two days."

"What does that mean?"

"I do not know."

"Did you tell his father?"

"I did not think it has anything to do with the dog barking."

"It may."

Emily went to the truck to check Mama and Okwy as they waited for Doctor. Outside, she told Mama about Obumneme's drawing.

"Go and bring it," Mama said to Emily.

Emily went inside and brought the notebook to Mama. As she opened it to show Mama, Okwy began to scream again, this time pointing at the notebook.

"It is the attack of the dwarfs," Mama said, looking at the drawing of tiny objects surrounding a small boy and a dog barking at one end. "We have to get Okwy out of here."

"Who are the dwarfs?"

"The mysterious servants of Eze Nri."

"What do they want?"

"They came to deliver a message."

"What message?"

"I don't know. I can't tell. But I know it is an important message."

"So what should we do?"

"Get a hotel room and stay there until we consult the oracle."

"In America?"

Up in the room, the doctor called Tessy to explain his delay in returning her page.

"Early this morning, my friend Onyebuchi had psychotic episodes. He was at the house screaming, 'Dwarfs, Dwarfs, they are everywhere. They are kicking me.' There were no dwarfs anywhere. His wife dialled 911 and he was brought to the hospital."

"Was he seeing them in the hospital?" asked Tessy.

"No, we actually discharged him this afternoon after he stabilized. But upon getting home, it started again. He has just been taken back into the psychiatric ward."

"Well, we've got a problem," said Tessy.

"What problem?"

"It seems the dwarfs are also in our home."

"What are you talking about?"

"Obumneme has been drawing them on his pad and Okwy, Emily's son, has been screaming since he got to our house. He would neither sit nor stand. He kept pointing at objects only he sees."

There was a chilly pause at the other end of the phone. It was clear that the doctor like a cricket had encountered in its hole something bigger than itself.

"Please take everyone to the Hilton on Sunset Boulevard. I will meet you there," Doctor said as he hung the phone.

A dejected doctor took a long walk to his car at each step wondering what could be amiss. If there was something he hated most, it was situations like this where his western education could not explain an African phenomenon. If it was only Onyebuchi that was seeing the dwarfs, he could have easily dismissed it. But for his son and the visiting son of his wife's sister to be seeing these same dwarfs was more than a coincidence.

He sat in his car and thought for a while. He wondered if he would see the same dwarfs when he gets home. He could not imagine what it would do to his reputation if he were to see the dwarfs and be as psychotic as Onyebuchi. For the first time, he examined what connected him to Onyebuchi for in that connection the solution to this mystery might be found.

It was two years ago that Onyebuchi brought wine to his house and presented a business proposal. Doctor had known him as an industrious Oba son and as his secretary at the Igbo Union of Southern Los Angeles. He had earned Doctor's respect and trust. But until then, they had not had any business dealings together.

"I want to establish a museum of African art," Onyebuchi said after eating kola and spiced peanut butter. "And I want you to be part of it. It will serve as a research outfit as well as a cultural centre. It will have a function hall, a library of African books and films, and a museum of ancient African arts. It will also serve as an outlet for the sale of modern African art."

"What part do you want me to play?" asked Doctor as he went through the written proposal.

"I want you to be part owner. I want you to invest in the project. I have a big function hall in downtown LA that I am modifying for this purpose. I need money to finish the work and also to go out in search of art pieces for the museum."

"And where will you find the art works?"

"In Africa."

"Isn't there a law against taking ancient artwork out of Africa?"

"When a cunning man dies, a cunning man buries him."

Doctor invested one hundred thousand dollars in the project. When it was opened last year, senators, congressmen and leading politicians in LA attended the opening ceremony. It got the endorsement of UCLA and raised doctor's profile within the political circle of California. In fact, he attributed his interest in politics at home to his adventure in the museum project.

A knock on the window of his car startled Doctor out of his thoughts. He looked up and it was Onyebuchi's wife.

"Is he alright?" asked doctor as he wound down his car window.

"He is doing ok," she said, "I just wanted to let you know something."

Doctor opened his car door and climbed out. He leaned on the car and listened.

"Last week, Onyebuchi came back from Senegal. He brought this ugly ngwu, sculpture with him that had fresh blood on it. I asked him why bring the ones with blood on them. I asked him if he was sure these new works he was bringing were not gods of some African people. He dismissed me as a closet heathen, "a superstitious hen," he said. "He was cleaning it in the garage when he started acting weird. I think what is happening to him has something to do with that ngwu."

"Are you sure he got it from Senegal?" asked doctor.

The direction of his query surprised Onyebuchi's wife. She wondered if doctor had come to the same conclusion all along.

"I don't know exactly where he got it from," confessed Onyebuchi's wife. "But I know the last time he travelled he went to Nigeria and then to Senegal."

"I am pretty sure it came from Nri," doctor said, emphatically. "Tomorrow, I will buy Onyebuchi an airline ticket and make sure he takes it back to Africa where it belongs."

At the airport were Onyebuchi's and Doctor's family; Tessy, her mother and Okwy. They had all come from the Hilton Hotel for the solemn event. Onyebuchi checked in his only luggage, the ngwu and was ready to board. He did not say a word all through the process. He did not hug his wife. He did not as much as wink a goodbye. He simply walked through the security checkpoint and headed for his departure gate.

As the family waited for the flight to take off, all eyes were on Obumneme's drawing pad. There was relief on everyone's face as he drew an airplane in the air and some dwarfs flying alongside its wings.

"Hurrah," said Okwy as he threw his right hand into the air in a high five gesture. Doctor caught Okwy's hand in mid-air, saying, "What do you say – we go to Disneyland and see Mickey Mouse."

Interview

Extract from an Interview with Sun Newspaper's Henry Akubuiro

1. It took you quite sometime after the publication of *Children of a Retired God* to come up with *This American Life Sef!* What happened in between?

Rudolf Okonkwo: What happened in between is called life. Life happened. Apart from changing diapers, making school runs, shuttles to piano lessons, birthday parties, play recitals, karate classes, soccer game, I also went to a seminary to become a pastor. I even started a church. It was a brand-new church, one that I built from the ground up. It required a lot of work. It is not like all these franchise churches that you see at every street corner, those ones they just hand you a template from the headquarters and you go to a storefront and replicate what has been done and perfected. In my own case, nobody told me what kind of wine to use for Holy Communion, what kind of gown to put on as the pastor or the kind of beard to grow. It is a tough world out there when you are on your own. To build up a congregation is not an easy task. I can tell you that I truly understand why those who made a success of that venture want to reward themselves with a private jet, big mansions all over the world and the numerous perks for being a General Overseer. In terms of the lifestyle of the likes of Bishop David

Oyedepo, Pastor Enoch Adeboye and Prophet T.B. Joshua, I failed in my church venture. And I understand my failure if that is what people call it. I failed mainly because I did not want to collect offerings and tithes from my congregation. I don't think it is fair. I think it is unethical. And as long as I have my congregation and as long as they keep growing and keep glowing in the spirit of the knowledge that we share, I consider myself a success.

Ok, before your readers run with this story—that was just an analogy. The seminary that I went to was the Western Connecticut State University where I obtained an MFA in Creative and Professional Writing- a kind of Theology, if you ask me. Anyway, after that, I started a church called Dr. Damages Show on SaharaTV. That was what happened. But because my first love is writing, it was inevitable that I would come back to it.

2. *This American Life Sef!* has a sarcastic title. What led you to write this book on the life of African immigrants in America?

Rudolf Okonkwo: When it comes to talking to my people, the Africans, I asked myself what is more effective? Is it to ask them to go to a mirror and count their teeth? We have tried that for a long time now but our experience showed that the object in the mirror is a virtual copy of the actual object with the right hand showing up as left. I said to myself, what about asking them to use their tongue to count their teeth? We have tried that and it has not worked very well. In fact, it has become a cliché. Moreover, the tongue has difficulty demarcating where one tooth ends and another begins. So, I felt the best way to reach my people is to tell them to use their teeth to count their tongue. It makes them pause immediately they hear it. And if you can get an African to pause, pause in the worship of their God to lift up the log of wood in front of them, pause in the worship of money, power, European soccer, then, half of your job is done.

I decided to put the book together as a complementary book to a tour of the US that I embarked on with Adeola Fayehun of *Keeping It Real with Adeola* in December 2015. The theme of the tour was, *This America Sef Tour*. So, it fitted well.

3. This book is a melding of essays and short stories. What's the sense behind this fusion?

Rudolf Okonkwo: The decision to fuss essays and fiction together is to capture the complete spectrum of African life in America. Essays based on real life of people have the limitations of giving you timelines and stamps that you cannot alter. Fiction gives you greater license to invent and reach corners that real life stories may not perfectly arrange in one particular life. In a short story you can integrate the experiences of two dozen people into one composite character. Another reason is that readers all over the world are drifting from fiction to non-fiction. In the case of Africans, books on how to achieve prosperity are doing well- just like religious book. So, we need to mash that up with fiction to bring our people back to the kind of reading culture we had in the 70s and 80s. A writer that does not know where his readers are is like a shepherd that does not know where his flocks are.

4. In the preface to the book, you penned thus: "But the debt that lives in whispers/ Is the debt of return/ It's one debt that is never forgiven". What are you driving at?

Rudolf Okonkwo: The debt of return is one that anyone who embarks on a journey owes the journey and the people he or she left behind. That is the reason for return tickets. People buy return ticket even when they do not know when they plan to return. But return they must. The demand to return is whispered into your ears by both men and spirits. Sometimes it is loud and sometimes it is a mere whisper. But it is always there. Our people say that the overall purpose of a journey is a return to where we came from. It is the ultimate challenge facing anyone who dares to leave the land of his or her birth. That question won't leave you alone until you return - whether in life or in death. So many return when they are dead. If you mention that reality to an African in America or anywhere considered "abroad", he or she will mutter, over my dead body. The smart answer, however, is to say, tufiakwa. Tufiakwa is a form of acknowledgment that it is a possibility that you do not wish for. But in matters of life and death, there is so little currency in what we wish. If sacrifices and supplications fail again and again, of what use is mere wishes from the perimeters of our minds? Thousands of return tickets go unused each year. It hunts those who made that purchase. You don't forgive yourself for not using it. And you don't forget it, either.

5. On your way to London, you encountered a Nigerian who said unflattering things about the USA. If you were to meet him again, what would you have told him?

Rudolf Okonkwo: If I meet that man again, I will apologize to him for thinking he was crazy when he was telling me that America was not a bed of roses. I will then give him an autographed copy of *This American Life Sef!* I will tell him not to worry about talking to others about it, that he can buy the book and give to people to read for themselves. You know, the dismissive way that I looked at him that day, I have received the same look from many people—maybe as a payback, I guess. I had looked at him and must have said to myself things like, "go sit down joor. Maybe you are one of the lazy types who do not want to work." I must have said in my mind, "maybe he has made it and has established himself well in Nigeria that he can afford to turn his back on America." I am now used to all those expressions of resentment and passive aggression. Mine is even worse because the first question that I get is the one that says: "if America is that bad, why are you still there?" The man I met on the plane didn't have to answer such a question. I still go about answering that question to people who are rightfully dissatisfied by whatever answer that I give, even when I explain that the goal of writing the book is not to discourage anyone from coming to America but to give people the tools they need to make informed decisions, to get prepared and give themselves a fighting chance.

6. In the book, you tell us that "The African man in America is confused". What's the extent of this confusion?

Rudolf Okonkwo: George Bernard Shaw said that there are two tragedies in life—one is getting what you want and the other is not getting what you want. We are familiar with the tragedy of not getting what we want. The most difficult one is the tragedy of getting what we want. The reason it is tougher is that "getting what you want" entails changing who you are. Nobody is ever fully prepared for it. You cannot be fully prepared for what you do not fully understand. It is also the reason fame is deadlier than poverty and inconspicuousness. For being in America, the African man changes. He can fight the change but America wins in the end. America changes the African man to the point that he will be confused about his identity. To understand that shifting identity is the first challenge- some do, some don't. I often quote that wise man who said that "those who are not lost in the understanding of their confusion are lost in confusion of their understanding." After you arrive at a convenient answer as to your identity, even if you come up with nonsense like Afropolitan, you still have to deal with your destiny. Without a clearly defined destination, there cannot be a satisfactory answer to the destiny question.

Some forms of confusion come from complex matters while some come from simple matters. For example, if you are not the head of the household by virtue of not being able to completely provide for the family, then what are you? If a phone call to the police can kick you out of the house you call "your house," is that house really yours? If you are a chief in your village but in America you are the one assigned the task of taking out the trash and walking the dog, how relevant is that your chieftaincy title?

At best, the longer you stay in America, the more you are a ghost of your former self. As you go from eating organic food to processed food, you evolve. Most African men end up like a bat- a mammal that flies but one that is not quiet an animal of the air or one of the land—a hybrid.

7. "Saving Mama Udoka" brings us home to the trajectory of the marriage institution. What is it about America that make African husbands in the US treat their wives like Mama Udoka? This theme echoes, too in "Before you Kill Your Wife".

Rudolf Okonkwo: Well, it is not as if African men in Africa are doing a lot better. While Nigeria is a failed nation that works for the very people who failed it, America is a developing nation constantly swinging like a pendulum from degradation to excellence in its quest to build a more perfect union. It follows that anyone within America goes through the mood.

Marriage is the most important challenge facing the African man in America. It is in marriage that all the information hidden in the African man's chromosomes emerge. For eight hours at work, the African man can swallow the cultural shock and navigate the cultural differences between him and America. He can compartmentalize the internalized lifestyle of his forefather for twelve hours at work. But once at home, the monsters crawl out. It is interesting how it all plays out. In their teens and 20s, you find the African man wanting to adopt, as much as possible, aspects of American cultures. In their 30s, they begin to doubt some of them that they find unpalatable. In their 40s, they begin to question most of them for being culturally incompatible. And in their 50s, they begin to resent most of them as cultural imperialism. In their 60s, the battle is over and the African man has come to terms with his defeat and will find solace in peripheral matters like western medicine, social amenities and any other convenience he could lay his hand on. At this point, the African man will swallow his indignation and raise a white flag.

The conflicts between the African man in America and his wife take place at the peak of this transformation. What is universally known is that the African woman in America has greater societal protection than the woman in Africa. Roles in families are different. In most cases, it is a reversal of what is obtainable in Africa. Usually it is all about money and the pressures associated with it. In America, the African woman is in a position to make more money than most African men. In most families, it turns things upside down. The African man must adjust accordingly or else, find himself at odd with American society. Those who have the temperament to adjust survive. For those who don't, they end up cooling off in various prisons across America.

During this trip I visited a friend's house and saw a microwave he bought from a trip to China. The microwave was in a box. I asked him why he has not brought it out and set it up. He said he intentionally left it in the box to avoid having his wife tell him to go and warm his own food when he returns from work. If my friend comes to America, he will be a dead man walking. In America his problem won't be small matter like having to go and warm his food. He will find himself literally and figuratively pounding yam with pestle and mortar while carrying the baby on his back. It is that brutal, the reversal of roles. Only the flexible survives. You are not just going to be flexible with the role you play, you also have to be flexible with career, with attitude and with expectations.

8. Contrary to what we think at home, this book has shown us that living in America has many downturns. The hyphenated Nigerian child you mentioned is one

disturbing example. Can you explain more?

Rudolf Okonkwo: When it is all said and done, the lasting contribution of the African man or woman's journey to America is to add to the gene pool of America. Majority of the African child born in America will not go back to Africa to live. It doesn't matter how many times African parents took them home for a visit. They are gone. It is the most difficult reality for many Africans in America to swallow. It doesn't matter what mansion you build in your country of origin. For most of them the journey back home ends when they come to bury their parents. This is another discussion that brings about 'tufiakwa' from Africans in America. Those deep in church will exclaim, "It is not my portion." But it was the portion of Italian, English, German, Irish, Russian and Jewish migrants that came before the Africans. That of Africans would not be different. An African child born in America is, for all intents and purposes, an American child. It is not just on paper, it is in fact. As long as he or she grew up in America, America will ooze out of the child. Unfortunately, there is nothing that African parents will have in Africa that will be more inviting than the aura of America. The way you have the lost children of Sudan is the way the African children being born in America today will become the lost children of Africa. As for the parents, when their family trees are drawn in Africa, after their names, a line will be drawn that will end there, indicating that nothing is known of his or her offspring. It is like the proverb that talked about washing ones hands to crack a kernel for a fowl.

9. The short story "A Kernel for a Fowl" is a story about unrequited love. What exactly spurred you to write it?

Rudolf Okonkwo: "A Kernel for a Fowl" builds on that challenge around finding love. It is not that there are not many African people in America for single Africans to choose from. It is that the spread of Africans due to the wideness of America makes it hard for people to meet people. Life in America can be isolating in nature. When you add that to the fact that America reshuffles class and status, it complicates what is usually a difficult task of finding a life partner. Add that to the prejudice that Africans in America already carry in their minds the way a snail carries a shell on its back and you begin to understand how tremendously challenging that act could be. Unrequited love can be the most painful experience anyone would go through. It can happen anywhere and to anybody. But if it happens to someone who has limited options, it is more devastating. Even though America is thousands of miles away from Africa, the influence of family members on decisions like marriage is still big. The prospective mother in-law is still a major player in the whole drama. The character in "A kernel for a fowl" found that out in a hard way.

10. In "The Butcher, the Surgeon and I", home is presented as "where you are stuck". I find this interesting. Can you elaborate from a diasporan perspective?

Rudolf Okonkwo: For most of us, despite our desires for a different outcome, we find ourselves stuck where we are. It may be as a result of work, a result of opportunities or a result of our inability to sell our home and move. There are several grandmothers who have made America home. It is not because they love it so much that they prefer it to their place of birth. Some are just stuck taking care of their grandchildren. There are so many Africans in America who feel that someone in their village is out to get them and to kill them. As a result, they have made America home. There are many Africans who for health reasons cannot afford to live in a different society other than America and are therefore forced by circumstances to make it their home. I know a man who cleaned out the money he has in his retirement account to build a house in his village only to get home and find out that there was no house. His siblings had simply spent the money and were sending him pictures of other people's homes under construction. He is essentially stuck in America. We struggle to get to that ideal place we call home, even when the ideal is ever changing. Often when we get to the place we imagine as the ideal home, we encounter its inadequacies and instantly we conceive a new place as a new ideal. Those who survive are the ones who manage to make a home out of the place they are stuck. That is why our romantic attachment to the place we were born, the place our placenta was buried is enduring. It is the only place we forgive of its inadequacies. We allow its illusory beauty to outshine its rugged reality.

Acknowledgements

Even though it was a last minute decision to put this book together in support of the *This America Sef Tour*, it still requires an army of people to make it happen. It includes people who worked on the manuscript, people who picked up my slack at every other station of my life while I worked on the manuscript and those who were cheering from the side.

Amongst those who read the manuscript are Kwesi 'Jahbeloved' Baako, Margret Mukami Kamau and Chika Oduah. Your perspectives have helped in a long way to shape my vision.

Cheering on the side is Okey Ndibe. Okay, sometimes he cheers from the ring, too. Though this is not what you had in mind, 'but heck, a man got to do what a man got to do.'

I must express my gratitude to my tour partner, Adeola Fayehun. If you had not signed up for this tour, this book may still have remained one of the stillborn. Your drive is a source of strength to anyone privileged to work with you.

To all those who have published my works in different columns over the years, I say thank you- McLord Obiorah of Nigeria & Africa magazine, Moe Ene of Kwenu.com, Chuck Odili of Nigeriaworld.com, Adekunle Philips of Nigeriavillagesquare.com, Alex Kabba of African-Abroad USA newspaper, Chido Nwangwu of USAfricaonline.com.

And of course, the big mogul himself, Omoyele Sowore of Saharareporters.com.

Some of the works in this book were once published in one form or the other by one or more of these chroniclers of our stories. They provided the vehicle that brought the tale to town.

I want to thank my wonderful mother-in-law, Gold Veronica Onwunyi, for being a wonderful mother to us all. She made it possible for me to disappear for a long time without wondering what happens to my two kids, Ijeamaka and Ogonna.

To my kids, Ijeamaka and Ogonna, thank you for understanding. Daddy is just trying to do better so that you will have a stronger shoulder to climb on.

To my beautiful wife, Edna: all these years, you have refused to be fatigued—not by dreams deferred, by promises unfulfilled or by follies enhanced by age. You are the editor-in-chief and the counsellor-in-chief. You are more than everything.

And to all the people who have read and responded in one way or the other to anything I have written—please, accept my appreciation.

Rudolf Ogoo Okonkwo is a Nigerian journalist and writer. He hosts the *Dr. Damages Show* on SaharaTV and writes a weekly column, *Correct Me If I'm Right,* for Saharareporters.com.

He has a Bachelor's degree in Engineering from the Federal University of Technology, Akure in Ondo State, Nigeria and an MFA in Professional and Creative Writing from Western Connecticut State University, Danbury, USA.

He is the author of a book of essays, *Children of a Retired God.* A chapter of his memoir, *Because I'm my Grandfather,* was a finalist in the 2010 John Guyon Literary Non-fiction Prize Competition. His short story, 'The Butcher, the Surgeon & Me,' was a finalist in Glimmer Train's 2009 Open Fiction Competition. He just finished work on his first novel, *Death on Mount Trashmore.*

www.ingramcontent.com/pod-product-compliance
Lightning Source LLC
Chambersburg PA
CBHW071259040426
42444CB00009B/1783